# The Word of God
## vs
# The Work of God
The Difference and The Relationship

# James Tawiah Mensah

Published by Gloripub
Printed in the U.S.A
Copyright © 2016
All rights reserved solely by the author. The author guarantees all contents are original and do not infringe upon legal rights of any other person or work. No part of this book may be reproduced in any form except for brief quotations in printed reviews, without the permission of the author

Unless otherwise stated, all Scripture quotations are taken from the *Holy Bible*, New International Version *(NIV)* Full Life Study Bible. Copyright 1985, 1995, 2002 by Zondervan Publishing House.
The article, 'The Word of God' (pages 1062, 1063) from the above Bible guided me on Chapter One, '*What is the Word of God?*' Author

Contact: *jamestawiahmensah@yahoo.com*

ISBN-13: 978-0-9976213-4-1
ISBN-10: 0997621346

*Also by James Tawiah Mensah*

- SUCCESS: WHAT IS IT ALL ABOUT?
- GIVING: WHAT IS IT ALL ABOUT?
- LOYALTY: WHAT IS IT ALL ABOUT?

*"Heaven and earth will pass away, but my **WORDS** will never pass away" (Matthew 24:35).*

# Table of Content

*Dedication  i*

*Acknowledgement  v*

*Foreword  ix*

*Prologue  xiii*

*What is the Word of God?  1*

*What is the Work of God?  27*

*What is the Difference?  57*

*What is the Relationship?  71*

*What is the Observation?  85*

*What is the Response?  99*

*Epilogue  109*

*Impressions About The Bible (Word Of God) By Some Prominent Persons:  117*

*Reference  121*

# Dedication

My beloved wife, Mrs. Martha Mensah, and the children—Dorinda Darley Mensah, Dennis Welbert Mensah, and Derrick Aklama Mensah.

# TO GOD BE THE GLORY

# Acknowledgement

My late parents, Mr. Abednego Aklama Mensah, and Mad. Christiana Charkuor Charway, whose words of wisdom and character shaped mine; my brothers, Rev. Michael Martey Mensah, Ghana and Nigeria; Mr. James Martey Mensah, Mr. William Mensah and sisters; late Ms. Adelaide Adoley Mensah, Ms. Belinda Marteykuor Mensah, Ms. Ruth Akweley Mensah, Ms. Letitia Agoyo Mensah and Ms. Alberta Abah Mensah, all in Ghana, whose contributions, in various times and ways, also helped to make me what I am today.

Rev. Benjamin Kwadjo Boakye, Senior Pastor, Ebenezer Assembly of God Church, Bronx, New York, USA, my present pastor, made me the Superintendent, Sunday School Department, and provided the tools needed to succeed. Rev. Emmanuel Yawson and Pastor Ignatius Kyereboah, Associate Pastors, Ebenezer Assembly of God Church, Bronx, New York, USA. My good buddies, Brother George Kwame Arkhurst and Minister Tony Aghamiogie and fellow Sunday School teachers, encouraged me in diverse ways.

Also, the students who listen to me every Sunday inspired me with their contributions in class. All Department leaders and entire members of Ebenezer Assembly of God Church, Bronx, New York, USA, gave me the opportunity to use my talent and gift to serve; Mr. Awuku Darko, Armor-bearer, Living Faith Ministry Int., Mount Vernon, New York, USA, and his wife, Sister Unity Agyeman, stood by me during the writing with words of encouragement.

Mr. and Mrs. Raymond and Abigail Kotei, West Haven, Connecticut, USA, my biggest fans; Mr. Joseph Nartey, my brother-in-law, Bronx, New York, USA; a very, very good friend, Pastor Isaac Twumasi, Ghana; Mr. Patrick Lucas Onasis Aryerh, Ghana, (aka P.L.O Aryerh); Mrs. Anna Christa Rawls Sackey, edited and wrote the foreword for *"Success: What is it all about?"* Rev. William Kanych, Senior Pastor, Faith Assembly of God, Yonkers, New York, USA, edited and wrote the foreword for *"Giving: What is it all about?"* Rev. Nancy Pierre, edited and wrote the foreword for

*"Loyalty: What is it all about?"* Pastor Kwame Acheampong, author, *"Fashion and Faith,"* and Ms. Joyce Ohene-Amoah, author, *"Building A Healthy Lasting Marriage,"* inspired me.

# Foreword

If anyone was asked to show God's power in this world, perhaps the WORD OF GOD which manifests in the WORK OF GOD might be the most authentic proof. Many of us are still inclined to think that God created the world in six days after which God's work came to a halt. This is a concept that many Christians, and even non-Christians, are skeptical of. Certainly not! God's work continues till today. Many authors tell their stories through the books they write. But this book tends to explore beyond any doubt how the WORD OF GOD and the WORK OF GOD are related to the each other and more so their differences. This book is not only to make us knowledgeable, but also to strengthen our relationship with God through His Word. In knowing the WORD OF GOD, we become invigorated to do the WORK OF GOD while working towards our individual salvation as well. The Bible declares that, "In the beginning was the Word, and the Word was with God, and the word was God...The WORD (OF GOD) became flesh and made his dwelling among us" (John 1:1, 14). This proclamation was in reference to Jesus Christ: the WORD OF GOD. Hence accepting Jesus Christ will rejuvenate anyone who decides to do the WORK OF GOD as John the Baptist did. John the Baptist indeed testified about Jesus, thus doing the WORK OF GOD.

God instructs us all to go into the world and preach the gospel as professed in the book of Mark (Mark 16:15). This, in essence, is doing the WORK OF GOD. Doing the WORK OF GOD as a preacher, a teacher, usher, a treasurer, a singer or a drummer, there is the demand that you must know the WORD OF GOD if you are doing it through God's calling. For God's Word is the standard for our lives, the compass we rely on for directions and the counsel we listen to for making decisions that are not only great, but wise. It is also, the benchmark we use for evaluating everything. Like Jesus said, "Everyone who hears these words of mine and puts them into practice is like a wise man who built his house on the rock" (Matthew 7:24 NIV). To become the authority of Christ on earth, we must become living carriers of God's word.

There is no one more vested in explaining the WORD OF GOD and the WORK OF GOD in details than Minister

## Foreword

James Mensah. He is a preacher and a teacher of teachers. I have known him for a decade now as the Sunday School Superintendent of the Ebenezer Assembly of God Church in the Bronx. In his class, he articulates the word of God fervently and unadulterated. In many instances, where discussions became very heated, he combines his theological experiences with the wisdom of God to explicitly explain the Bible. This translates into his Sunday School lessons that are not only broad, but relevant to shaping one's Christian astute. He strives to create an enabling environment where students in his class will have the opportunity to express their knowledge of God's word. He will rank among the top 2% of Sunday School Superintendents I have encountered in my Christian life.

This book will motivate every believer in Christ, to love, to learn and to live the WORD OF GOD like never before. God's Word is not meant only for studies to increase our knowledge, but a conviction to put it into practice as we perform God's work. It is written to urge anyone who has doubts about the authority of God's WORD in His WORK. Jesus Christ used the word to heal the sick, to chastise the devil, to calm the raging sea, to raise the dead and to cast out demons. This is how the WORD OF GOD comes alive in the WORK OF GOD. Minister Mensah, in this book, narrates how much we need to know WORD OF GOD to do the WORK OF GOD. This interestingly enough, depicts the clear-cut difference and the relationship between the WORD OF GOD and the WORK OF GOD. Obtaining a copy of this book will also bring to your realization that Christ's use of the spoken word in His work whiles here on Earth, is a means to justify the power of God's word.

*Leeford H. Dufe,*
*(High School Teacher & a Doctoral Candidate)*
*Bethel, Connecticut,*
*United States of America.*

# Prologue

*"Heaven and earth will pass away, but my <u>WORDS</u> will never pass away"* (Matthew 24:35).

He is a very tall and lanky person. As a result, he stands out a lot among his peers as far as height is concerned. His steps are wide as he enters the sanctuary at a speed beyond normal. The usual seriousness he wears on his face as he enters the sanctuary sometimes scares me. I seldom see him smile. His habit of coming in late coveted my attention. He doesn't participate in Sunday School Bible studies, where he would get the opportunity to ask questions, and his questions would be answered. So after careful consideration and consultation with my fellow teachers, we concluded he must be told of this shortcoming. Though he is as young as my child, yet I did not want to approach him over this issue, even though I believed it would be of great benefit to him should I make this attempt.

## The Word of God vs. the Work of God

For this particular reason, one day, I mustered up courage from nowhere and confronted him. I did it in a manner deemed fit and appropriate. I pulled him away from the rest of the congregation and began thus:

"I have observed that you usually come to church when Sunday School had far gone into its allotted time, thinking and expecting that you would quietly join your friends in your class. Unfortunately, you do not go so you can study the WORD OF GOD. You rather choose to go straight and check the instruments." I paused there to gather some more courage. Then I spoke further with this assessment: "The strong lure of these musical instruments will not conjure any automatic spirituality in you. No, it does not work like that. Yet ignorantly, you are trading all this important possession with the pull from these instruments, a pull that you are finding very difficult to resist."

"I assume you equate the importance of what you do - checking the instruments one after another - with studying and knowing God's word through scriptures. I know you never stepped back to reconsider this assumption. But I want you to know that the WORD OF GOD and the WORK OF GOD are related; a fact that cannot be denied at all. Yet, they are worlds apart in difference. It will be greatly helpful for you if you would adhere more to His WORD than to the WORK you do at the church. For you can delegate someone to do the WORK in your stead, but when it comes to studying His WORD, you cannot," I added. Studying the WORD OF GOD would draw you nearer to the Holy Spirit and strengthen you in trying times. It would help to keep your character in check. Remember it was pride that caused the fall of Satan and music is his domain. "I should be glad if you would give this discussion a serious thought. Have a good day," I concluded. He nodded in response and thanked me. We parted then with a friendly good-bye.

For the first time he exposed this uncommon smile. I was impressed and humbled by his humility that day. I was convinced beyond any reasonable doubt he had accepted my counseling. His demeanor spoke volume, and I was totally convinced to see him a changed person as the following Sundays ensued. Instead of the change I expected from him, he registered what would mark the beginning of a journey I would never have comprehended to travel. This young man is not, and will not be the only one caught in such a trap. Many long-serving Christians are caught in this web of ignorance too. And some ministers of God are no exception to this course. Mere negligence is the culprit on the part of ministers that do nothing about addressing this issue.

It is unfortunate we equate the WORD OF GOD with the WORK OF GOD. There is this assumption among church members that they are the same, therefore must be treated equally. In light of this assumption, while the WORD OF GOD is being studied, preached, and discussed in the sanctuary, some Christians - even those matured with responsible positions - just leave to go do the WORK OF GOD. As we do the WORK, instead of studying the WORD, we are thrilled to be serving God. We think we will mature. We think we are obeying the exhortation the LORD Almighty gave Joshua when He said,

> Do not let this book of the Law (the WORD OF GOD) depart from your mouth, meditate on it day and night, so that you may be careful to do everything written in it. Then you will be prosperous and successful (Joshua 1:8).

The WORD OF GOD and the WORK OF GOD are so closely related that without the adequate acquisition of the needed knowledge, we might be compelled to put them on the same scale. There are many Christians who cannot comprehend the idea that they are way apart like the distance between the east and the west. The lack of this knowledge is causing some believers to 'perish' or remain immature in the things of God. The LORD exposed this hidden fact to me and laid it upon my heart as a burden. The burden to explore the Bible, examine its content, extract the difference and relationship regarding the subject under discussion and then extend the truth that I will find to my fellow Christians to live the life God intended for us. It is so exciting to embark on this project. I should be pleased if you would accompany me on this journey to unveil this truth and help me make it known to all.

*James Tawiah Mensah*

# ONE

## What is the Word of God?

*"The <u>WORD</u> became flesh and made his dwelling among us. We have seen his glory, the glory of the One and Only, who came from the Father, full of grace and truth"* (John 1:14).

The Bible is the total embodiment of what we, Christians, call the WORD OF GOD. It is the standard with which the authenticity of any word or message that might come from outside of it is checked. These are words or messages, which could be claimed to have come from God. God speaks His mind to His people through the Bible. The *New International Bible Dictionary* explain

Thus, the WORD OF GOD is the fundamental aspect of God's self-revelation, for by his word he makes known who he is, what he is like, and what his will is for the world (Tenney, 1963)

Through the pages of the Bible, the people of God get the chance to know Him and His ways. Dr. Williams described the chance for this knowledge as

> The cry of the heart is for finding God, beholding Him, coming even into His presence. From the divine side, the Scriptures (WORD OF GOD) depict God as supremely desirous that His people shall know Him (Williams, 1996).

The prophet Jeremiah also confirmed God calling us to Himself and His WORD:

> the LORD says: Let not the wise boast of his wisdom or the strong man boast of his strength or the rich man boast of his riches, but let him who boasts boast about this: that he understands and knows me, that I am the LORD, who exercises kindness, justices and righteousness on earth, for these I delight,' declares the LORD (Jeremiah 9:23, 24).

This magnificent book warranted its protection from any human encroachment when it said:

## What is the Word of God?

> I warn everyone who hears the WORDS of the prophecy of this book: If anyone adds anything to them, God will add to him plagues described in this book. And if anyone takes WORDS away from this book of prophecy, God will take away from him his share in the tree of life and in the holy city, which are described in this book (Revelation 22:18, 19).

Its content was revealed through the medium of human endeavor; human beings who were inspired by the infallible God Himself. So, it is exciting to know that the origin of the WORD OF GOD is not with man and his knowledge and intelligence, but with God Almighty. And with this in mind, Peter boldly proclaimed in his second letter to its recipients, saying,

> Above all, you must understand that no prophecy of Scripture (WORD OF GOD) came about by the prophet's own interpretation. For prophecy never had its origin in the will of man, but men spoke from God as they were carried along by the Holy Spirit (2 Peter 1:20, 21).

Paul also emphasized the inspiration behind the WORD OF GOD through the second letter he penned to Timothy, his spiritual son. He stated,

All scripture (WORD OF GOD) is God-breathed and useful for teaching, rebuking, correcting and training in righteousness, so that the man of God may be thoroughly equipped for every good work (2Timothy 3:16, 17).

As we have ascertained the fact that the WORD OF GOD is God-inspired, let us attempt to look at its three dimensions: (1) **the Character,** (2) **the Ability** and (3) **the Believer's Response.**

## (1) THE CHARACTER OF THE WORD OF GOD

The WORD OF GOD - or the WORD of the LORD as alternatively used in the Bible - refers to various scenarios. Sometimes, it is simply referred to as the WORD. But the WORD OF GOD came to us through different human means spanning a period of about a thousand and four hundred years. And they are as the following: -

**(a)** The words God spoke directly to Adam and Eve are the WORD OF GOD. From the dust of the ground, God formed man. He planted a garden in the east, in Eden. He put man there and gave him instructions to take care of it.

And the LORD God commanded the man, "You are to eat from any tree in the garden; but from the tree of the knowledge of good and evil, for when you eat of it you will surely die" (Genesis 2:16,17).

When Cain and Abel had offered sacrifices to the LORD, Abel found favor as a result of the items he presented because God considered them appreciable. Jealousy crept into Cain's heart. He resented his brother, and finally, he killed him. The book of Genesis recorded the LORD speaking directly to Cain:

> Then the LORD said to Cain, "Why were you angry? Why is your face downcast? If you do what is right, will you not be accepted? But if you do not do what is right, sin is crouching at your door; it desires to have you, but you must master it (Genesis 4:6, 7).

The narrative of Noah and the building of the magnificent ark is another example we will consider God speaking His word. This event of building the ark and flooding of the then world was as a result of prevailing wickedness. The 'sons of God' saw that the daughters of men were very beautiful. They sought and had children through them. Every thought of the products from these unions was inclined to wickedness and evil beyond comprehension. Later, when God saw what was happening, He regretted He created man. He took a decision to destroy the earth with a flood; man and any other thing that has breath. The LORD, therefore, requested Noah to build an ark. When he finished building the ark,

> The LORD then said to Noah, "Go into the ark, you and your whole family, because I have found you righteous in this generation. Take with you seven of every clean animal, a male and its mate, and two of every kind of unclean animal, a male and its mate, and also seven of every kind of bird, male and female, to keep their various kinds alive throughout the earth. Seven days from now I will send rain the earth for forty days and forty nights, and I will wipe from the face of the earth every living creature I have made (Genesis 7:1-4).

The LORD also spoke to Abraham, after He had called him from among his family and friends.

> The LORD had said to Abram, "Leave your country, your people and your father's household and go to a land I will show you. I will make you into a great nation and I will bless you; I will make your name great, and you will be a blessing. I will bless those who bless you, and whoever curses you I will curse; and all people on earth will be blessed through you" (Genesis 12:1-3).

**(b)** Jesus was another source from which we received the WORD OF GOD. The words He spoke to His disciples were also classified as the WORD OF GOD. In fact, He was God Himself in human body. The Apostle explained the mystery this way,

> In the beginning was the Word, and the Word was with God, and the Word was God…The Word became flesh and made his dwelling among us. We have seen his glory, the glory of the One and Only, who came from the Father, full of grace and truth (John 1:1, 14).

Luke, without mincing words, said Jesus spoke the WORD OF GOD to His disciples.

> One day as Jesus was standing by the Lake of Gennesaret with people crowding around him and listening to the WORD OF GOD, he saw at the water's edge two boats, left there by the fishermen, who were washing their nets (Luke 5:1, 2).

Because of Jesus' divine authority, which He claimed "…in heaven and on earth has been given to me" (Matthew 28:18), He doesn't precede His statements with 'the LORD says.' He showed this authority when He said,

> I tell you the truth, until heaven and earth disappear, not the smallest letter, not the least stroke of a pen, will by any means disappear from the Law (the WORD OF GOD) until everything is accomplished (Matthew 5:18).

He went on to say:

> …I tell you that unless your righteousness surpasses that of the Pharisees and teachers of the law, you will certainly not enter the kingdom of heaven (Matthew 5:20).

Continuing with,

> …tell[ing] you the truth, some who are standing here will not taste death before they see the kingdom of God come with power (Mark 9:1).

Further, He claimed,

> I tell you the truth, whoever hears my WORD and believes in him who sent me has eternal life and will not be condemned; he has crossed over from death to life (John 5:24).

**(c)** In the same way, God spoke through the prophets of old, the likes of Ezekiel, Jeremiah, Haggai, Amos, Hosea, etc.

These prophets prefaced their messages with; "This is what the LORD says," "The word of the LORD came to me," or something similar. In this manner, what came to the recipients - the WORD OF GOD - came through the breath or the Spirit of God Himself. The following are some examples:

## (i) Ezekiel

The word of the LORD came to me: "Son of man, take a stick of wood and write on it, 'Belonging to Judah and the Israelites associated with him. Then take another stick of wood, and write on it, 'Ephraim's stick, belonging to Joseph and all the house of Israel associated with him. Join them together into one stick so that they will become one in your hand (Ezekiel 37:15-17).

## (ii) Jeremiah

This is what the LORD Almighty says: 'In this place, desolate and without men and women or animals- in all its towns there will again be pastures for shepherds to rest their flocks. In the towns of the hill country of the western foothills and of the Negev, in the territory of the Benjamin, in the villages around Jerusalem and in the towns of Judah, flocks will again pass under the hands of the one who counts them,' says the LORD (Jeremiah 33:12, 13).

## (iii) Haggai

This is what the LORD Almighty says: "Give careful thought to your ways. Go up into the mountains and bring down timber and build the house, so that I may take pleasure in it and be honored: say the LORD (Haggai 1:7).

## (iv) Amos

This is what the LORD says: "As a shepherd saves from the lion's mouth only two leg bones or a piece of an ear, so will Israelites be saved, those in Samaria sit on the edge of their beds and in Damascus on their couches (Amos 3:12).

## (v) Hosea

Hear the word of the LORD, you Israelites, because the LORD has a charge to bring against you who live in the land: "There is no faithfulness, no love no acknowledgement of God in the land. There is only cursing, lying and murder, stealing and adultery; they break bounds and bloodshed follows bloodshed (Hosea 4: I, 2).

**(d)** The Apostles spoke the WORD OF GOD. Though they did not proceed what they said with 'The Lord says,' or similar prefaces, yet their words carried the same authority. Before their hearers, they proclaimed the WORD OF GOD with the intensity it deserved. For example, during a sermon he preached in Pisidian Antioch, Paul made this assertion. Luke recorded it in Acts thus:

> On the next Sabbath, almost the whole city gathered to hear the WORD of the Lord…Then Paul and Barnabas answered them boldly: "We had to speak the WORD OF GOD to you first. Since you reject it and do not consider yourself worthy of eternal life, we now turn to the Gentiles…" The WORD of the Lord spread through the whole region (Acts 13:44, 46, 49).

In his first letter to the Thessalonian believers, Paul further made an authoritative claim. The WORD proceeding out of his mouth must be considered as that of God. He said,

> …we also thank God continually because you received the WORD OF GOD, which you heard from us, you accepted it not as the word of men, which is at work in you who believe (1 Thessalonians 2:13).

**(e)** Finally, let's consider the proclamation from the pulpits by preachers and prophets and other ministers of the gospel in the church today. The authority of their proclamation might not be at par with the Scriptures though, yet they are considered the WORD OF GOD they (preachers, prophets, etc.) prayerfully sought God's guidance through the scriptures to reach His people. But such preaching from preachers and word from the prophet should not be received independent of the written WORD OF GOD, which is the Bible. For example, Paul encouraged Timothy in the second letter to him.

> Preach the WORD; be prepared in season and out of season; correct, rebuke and encourage - with great patience and careful instruction (2 Timothy 4:2).

Peter, in support of Paul's assertion, expressed in his first letter thus:

> For, "All men are like grass, and all their glory is like the flowers of the field; the grass withers and the flowers fall, but the WORD of the Lord stands forever." And this is the WORD that was preached to you (1:24, 25).

From the above exposition of facts, we are able to identify the first dimension of the WORD OF GOD, which is its character. They - God, Jesus, the prophets, the apostles, and the preachers from behind our pulpits - spoke, and continue to speak, what Christians consider to be the infallible WORD OF GOD. Now, with this knowledge intact, let us look at the ability of the WORD OF GOD, which is its second dimension. It is very crucial for every believer to be aware of and appreciate the ability of the WORD OF GOD.

## (2) THE ABILITY OF THE WORD OF GOD

The ability of the WORD OF GOD cannot be overemphasized. The Psalmist claims its firm standing in heaven (Psalm 119:89). The WORD OF GOD is active, creative, and effective. It accomplishes the purposes for which it is proclaimed on this earth too. The LORD Himself confirmed this through the Prophet Isaiah that just

> As the rain and the snow come down from heaven, and do not return to it without watering the earth and making it bud and flourish, so that it yields seed for the sower and bread for the eater, so is my WORD that goes out of my mouth: It will not return to me empty, but will accomplish what I desire and achieve the purpose for which I sent it (Isaiah 55:10, 11).

The WORD OF GOD remains the only source of power to redeem the human race from the bondage of sin and also liberate from the trammels of ignorance. Consider its ability in these diverse ways: -

(a)  **The WORD OF GOD** has the ability to create. From the Genesis account of creation, all that God made came into being through His spoken word.

> And God said, "Let the there be light and there was light…
>
> Let there be an expanse between the waters to separate water from water
>
> Let the water under the sky be gathered to one place and let the dry ground appear… (Genesis 1: 3, 6, 9).

The Psalmist supports the Genesis account with a proclamation saying "By the WORD of the LORD were the heavens made, their starry host by the breath of his mouth" (Psalm 33:6).

The Hebrews author substantiated this proclamation in order to give credence to the creative power of the WORD OF GOD. He wrote that, "By faith we understand that the universe was formed at God's command (WORD OF GOD), so that what is seen was not made out of what was visible" (Hebrews11:3).

**(b)** **The WORD OF GOD** has the ability to sustain creation. In the words of the Psalmist,

> He sends his command to the earth; his WORD runs swiftly. He spreads the snow like wool and scatters the frost like ashes. He hurls down his hail like pebbles. Who can withstand his icy blasts? He sends his WORD and melts them; he stirs up his breezes, and the waters flow (147:15-18).

In book of Hebrews too, God is "sustaining all things by his powerful WORD…" (1:3). Apostle Paul confirmed to the Colossians as Jesus being the WORD OF GOD when he said, "He is before all things, and in him all things hold together" (Colossians 1:17).

**(c)** **The WORD OF GOD** has the ability to dispense grace, enablement, and illumination so the believer can mature in the faith, in the walk with and commitment to Christ. The prophet Isaiah painted a perfect picture when he wrote that:

> As the rain and the snow come down from heaven, and do not return to it without watering the earth and making it bud and flourish, so that it yields seed for the sower and bread for the eater, so is my WORD that goes out of my mouth. (Is. 55:10, 11)

will cause the believer to spiritually 'bud and flourish.'

Peter declared the same sentiments when he intimated that "Like newborn babies, crave pure spiritual milk (WORD OF GOD), so that by it you may grow up in your salvation …" (1 Peter 2:2).

**(d)** **The WORD OF GOD** has the ability to help us fight Satan; the archenemy of the believer and the accuser of brethren. Paul urged the believers in Ephesus to "Take the helmet of salvation and the sword of the Spirit, which is the WORD OF GOD" in pursuit of the Christian journey (Ephesians 6:17). And this message has descended through the corridors of time to our generation.

Before He began His earthly ministry, Jesus fasted for forty days and forty nights. The Bible says He was hungry yet, He was led by the Holy Spirit to the desert to be tempted. For three times, Satan tempted Jesus. In all, Jesus invoked nothing but the WORD OF GOD to overcome him from all his attempts.

> Jesus answered, "It is written: 'Man does not live on bread alone, but every WORD (OF GOD) that comes from the mouth of God'" … "It is also written: 'Do not put the Lord your God to test'" … "Away

from me, Satan! For it is written: 'Worship the Lord your God and serve him only'" (Matthew 4: 4, 7, 10).

(e) **The WORD OF GOD** has the ability to transform lives that are perceived to be hopeless to be hopeful. For example, can transform from drug pushers to truth preachers. Paul is typical example; a murderer to a minister of the gospel. Apostle Peter unapologetically created awareness to this effect. He boldly proclaimed that "you have been born again, not of perishable seed, but of imperishable, through the living and enduring WORD OF GOD" (1Peter 1:23).

James echoed Peter's sentiment as he wrote to the early believers. He made them to be aware that,

> He chose to give us birth through the word of truth (WORD OF GOD), that we might be a kind of first fruits of all he created (James 1:18).

And Paul did not fail to remind Timothy

> how from infancy you have known the holy Scriptures (WORD OF GOD) which are able to make you wise for salvation through a faith in Christ Jesus (2 Timothy 3:15).

**(f)** **The WORD OF GOD** has the ability to judge the believer. Jesus plainly said, "There is a judge for the one who rejects me and does not accept my WORDS; that very WORD which I spoke will condemn him at the last day" (John 12:48).

The Hebrews writer augmented Jesus' argument with this assertion;

> For the WORD OF GOD is living and active. Sharper than any double-edged sword, it penetrates even to dividing soul and spirit, joints and marrow, it judges the thoughts and attitudes of the heart (Hebrews 4:12).

The prophets who came before Jesus, and later on, the apostles declared messages of God's judgment and condemnation through His words.

## (3) THE BELIEVER'S RESPONSE TO THE WORD OF GOD

The testimonies of those whose lives experienced drastic and dramatic change through the WORD OF GOD are very strong and certain. But since believers with different backgrounds had accepted Jesus as Lord and Savior, so will the responses to the WORD OF GOD be, definitely varying from person to person. For this reason, the Bible explicitly cautions how the believer should respond to it. And it will be beneficial if the believer would heed this caution. In fact, Jesus assured those who believed in Him that "If you hold on to my teaching (the WORD OF GOD), you are really my disciples. Then you will know the truth (the WORD OF GOD), and the truth will set you free" (John 8:31, 32). These responses should be: -

## (a) Listen to the **WORD OF GOD**

The only way the believer can mature in relation to God and to fellow brethren is to hear the WORD OF GOD. It's therefore incumbent upon the believer to draw nearer to the WORD OF GOD as much as possible. For "faith comes from hearing the message, and the message is heard through the word of Christ" (Roman 10:17).

> My son, pay attention to what I say; listen closely to my WORDS. Do not let them out of your sight, keep them within your heart (Proverbs 4:20, 21).

> Hear the WORD of the LORD, you rulers of Sodom; listen to the law of our God (Isaiah 1:10).

> ...Hear the WORD of the LORD, all you people of Judah who come through these gates to worship the LORD (Jeremiah 7:2).

## (b) Take the WORD OF GOD

Just hearing the WORD OF GOD is not enough for the believer. It must be taken to heart too. Paul praised the Corinthian church "that you are a letter (the WORD OF GOD) from Christ, the result of our ministry, written not with ink but with the Spirit of the living God, not on tablets of stone but on tablets of human hearts" (2 Corinthians 3:3).

> Others, like seed sown on good soil, hear the WORD, accept it, and produce a crop - thirty, sixty or even hundred times what was sown (Mark 4:20).

> Those who accepted his message (WORD OF GOD) were baptized, and about three thousand were added to their number that day (Acts 2:41).

## (c) Keep the WORD OF GOD

The only way the believer can fend off the enemy is by keeping the WORD OF GOD at all times. Memorization is one of the best, if not the best. Meditation is another alternative. I believe the devil is not scared of us but the WORD OF GOD, which is the sword in the armory of God

> I have hidden your WORD in my heart that not sin against you (Psalm 119:11).

> I tell you the truth, if anyone keeps my WORD, he will never see death (John 8:51).

## (d) Appreciate the WORD OF GOD

The WORD OF GOD cannot effectively manifest in our lives if we do not show the appreciation it deserves. The WORD OF GOD is life and full of hope, and the believer's failure to give it its due diligence would be detrimental in the Christian journey.

> I hate double-minded men, but I love your law (Psalm 119:113).

> If anyone is ashamed of me and my WORDS, the Son of Man will be ashamed of him when he comes in his glory and in the glory of the Father and of the holy angels (Luke 9:26).

## (e) Understand the WORD OF GOD

It is very important for every Christian to understand the WORD OF GOD in today's world, most especially. The Bible says, in the last days many false prophets will arise, giving interpretations that will suit what they stand for. We could easily fall victims to such connivance if we do not adequately understand the WORD OF GOD.

> But the one who received the seed that fell on good soil is the man who hears the WORD and

understands it. He produces a crop yielding a hundred, sixty or thirty times what was sown (Matthew 13:23).

Then he opened their minds so they could understand the Scriptures (WORD OF GOD) (Luke 24:45).

Now the Bereans were of more noble character than the Thessalonians, for they received the message with great eagerness and examined the Scriptures (WORD OF GOD) every day to see if what Paul said was true (Acts 17:11).

## (f)  Obey the WORD OF GOD

On many occasions, we allow the prevailing circumstances to influence and inform our decisions, instead of relying on the WORD. At the end of the day we fail miserably. David succinctly said the WORD OF GOD is the light on our path and a lamp to our feet. It is a good piece of advice we should not ignore.

>Samuel replied: 'Does the LORD delight in burnt offerings and sacrifices as much as in obeying the voice of the LORD? To obey is better than sacrifice, and to heed is better than the fat of rams' (1 Samuel 15:22).

Trust in the LORD with all your heart and lean not on your own understanding; in all your ways acknowledge him, and he will make your paths straight (Proverbs 3: 5, 6).

If you are willing and obedient, you will eat the best from the land, but if you resist and rebel, you will be devoured by the sword. For the mouth of the LORD has spoken (Isaiah 1:19).

Do not merely listen to the WORD, and so deceive yourselves. Do what it says. Anyone who listens to the WORD but does not do what it says is like a man who looks at his face in a mirror and after looking at himself, goes away and immediately forgets what he looks like (James 1:22-24).

## (g) Handle the WORD OF GOD

Curious people who would want to know why we believe what we believe. They would therefore bombard us with many questions. These seekers must not be left in a state of oblivion. The only way out is to perfectly handle the WORD OF GOD with clear explanation so they can walk away blessed.

Do your best to present yourself to God as one approved, a workman who does not need to be ashamed and who correctly handles the WORD of truth (2Timothy 2:15).

Always be prepared to give an answer to everyone who asks you to give the reason for the hope that you have. But do this with gentleness and respect (1 Peter 3:15).

## (h) Proclaim the WORD OF GOD

Jesus purposely and intentionally commissioned the Christian to go out there and proclaim the WORD OF GOD. How would they hear if no one proclaims it? This is where we fit in the equation.

> Stand at the gate of the LORD'S and there proclaim this message: 'Hear the word of the LORD, all you people of Judah who came through these gates to worship the LORD (Jeremiah 7:2).

> What I tell you in the dark, speak in the daylight; what is whispered in your ears, proclaim from the roofs (Matthew 10:27).

> That which was from the beginning, which we have heard, which we have seen with our eyes, which we

have looked at and our hands have touched – this we proclaim concerning the Word of life (1 John 1:1).

Those who had been scattered preached the WORD wherever they went. Philip went down to a city in Samaria and proclaimed the Christ there (Acts 8:4, 5).

From the preceding effort, we have been able to establish the three characteristics of the WORD OF GOD. And we have considered these characteristics too. Now let us proceed on with finding the truest meaning of the WORK OF GOD, and what it entails. We would realize the WORK OF GOD is more than what we have perceived it to be over the many years we have been Christians.

The Word of God vs. the Work of God

# TWO

## What Is the Work of God?

*"Whatever you do, <u>WORK</u> at it with all your heart, as working for the Lord, not for men, since you know that you will receive an inheritance from the Lord as a reward. It is the Lord Christ you are serving" (Colossians 3:23, 24).*

Whenever the WORK OF GOD is mentioned, its understanding is sorrowfully narrowed and confined to the church premises. It is believed that once God's name is attached to it then, it must be done only in His 'house.' At worst, this is the notion many church folks have been peddling around. But from the Bible's perspective, the WORK OF GOD covers a parameter broader than one can imagine. That is to say, it extends beyond the four walls of a church building. In fact, the

WORK OF GOD is more visible outside the church building than it is within. That was why Paul drew Timothy's attention to this trustworthy saying. He said, "Here is a trustworthy saying: If anyone sets his heart on being an overseer (doing the WORK OF GOD), he desires a noble task" (1Timothy 3:1). To make it more appealing wherever it is done, Jesus appealed to the disciples to "…let your light shine before men, that they may see your good deeds (the WORK OF GOD) and praise your Father in heaven" (Matthew 5:16). "Good deeds" was what Jesus entrusted to the care of the disciples before ascending to heaven. He commissioned them to

> Go into all the world and preach the good news to all creation. Whoever believes and is baptized will be saved, but whoever does not believe will be condemned (Mark 16:15, 16).

To successfully and fearlessly execute Jesus' work, the disciples needed to be endowed with a higher power. They were going to pit their strength "against the rulers, against the authorities, against the powers of this dark world and against the spiritual forces of evil in the heavenly realms" (Ephesians 6:12). This task was, and will not be an easy one, and Jesus knew it. Jesus then commanded His disciples: "Do not leave Jerusalem, but wait for the gift my Father promised, which you heard me speak about" (Acts 1:4). Then afterwards, He instructed them again with these:

> But you shall receive power when the Holy Spirit comes on you, and you will be my witnesses in <u>Jerusalem</u>, and <u>all Judea and Samaria</u>, and <u>to the ends of the world</u> (Acts 1:8).

When they had received this power, they went out from the upper room where they were hiding and began to preach the gospel at the possibility of losing their lives. The Apostles defied the authorities of the day and propagated this truth with the boldness and confidence it deserved. The Bible says, thousands believed and were added to their number. So in order to tackle all the areas the WORK OF GOD would cover, let us also divide it into three categories as the following: **(1) the Family *(Jerusalem)*, (2) the Church *(Judea and Samaria)* and (3) the Community *(the ends of the earth)*.**

## (1) THE WORK OF GOD IN THE FAMILY (JERUSALEM)

The family is a sacred institution, and God holds its success so dear to His heart. As a result, He said, "For this reason a man shall leave his father and mother and be united to his wife and the two shall be one flesh" (Genesis 2:24). Then they will "…Be fruitful and increase in number; fill the earth and subdue it..." (Genesis 1:26). So, "...what God has joined together, let no man separate" (Matthew 19:6). The family is one of the first human institutions, if not the first, God instituted. God ordained it Himself to be the foundation upon which every community is to be built and to be the foundation upon which every society should thrive. In fact, this is an institution whose definition cannot and must not be altered, or any attempt be made to. A change to its definition and functions will wipe out the human race and cause civilization to cease. Dysfunction in a family has dire consequences. It inflicts wounds of greater dimension on its victims than any known affliction, sometimes affecting succeeding generations. And the scars from these wounds stay for a long time. Therefore, each believer in this institution has a fundamental and a sacred role to play as outlined by the Bible so it would succeed. They are as:- **(a) A Father, (b) A Mother** and **(c) A Child.**

### (a) Doing the WORK OF GOD as a Father:-

Every home needs a father. The basic duties of a father cannot be traded with any other thing. A father has special roles to play in the lives of his children. Therefore, his absence in the family creates chaos and confusion. So, whatever the father does is the WORK OF GOD assigned to him. He is required to perform his duties as a father in these ways: -

## (i) To Teach

Fix these words of mine in your heart and mind; tie them as symbols on your hands and bind them on your foreheads. Teach them to your children, talking about them when you sit at home and when you walk along the road, when you lie down and when you get up (Deuteronomy 11:18, 19).

## (ii) To Lead

He must manage his own family well and see that his children obey him with proper respect (1Timothy 3:4).

But as for me and my household, we will serve the LORD (Joshua 24:15).

## (iii) To Provide

If anyone does not provide for his relatives, and especially his immediate family, he has denied the faith and is worse than an unbeliever (1Timothy 5:8).

## (iv) To Train

Folly is bound up in the heart of a child, but the rod of discipline will drive it far from him (Proverbs 22:15).

Train a child in a way he should go, and when he is old he will not turn from it (Proverbs 22:6).

Fathers, do not exasperate your children, instead, bring them up in the training and instruction of the Lord (Ephesians 6:4).

**(v)  To Love**
Husbands, love your wives, just as Christ loved the church and gave himself up for her to make her holy, cleansing her by the washing with water through the word… (Ephesians 5:25, 26).

In this same way, husbands ought to love their wives as their own bodies. He who loves his wife loves himself (Ephesians 5:28).

Husbands, love your wives and do not be harsh with them (Colossians 3:19).

**(vi)  To Advise**

My son, keep your father's commands and do not forsake your mother's teaching. Bind them upon your heart forever, fasten them around your neck (Proverbs 6:20).

A gentle answer turns away wrath, but a harsh word stirs up anger (Proverbs 15:1)

Remember your Creator in the days of your youth, before the days of trouble come and the years approach when you will say, 'I find no pleasure in them' (Ecclesiastes 12: 1).

**(vii) To Please**

By myself I can do nothing; I judge only as I hear, and my judgment is just, for I seek not to please myself but him who sent me (John 5:30).

**(b) Doing the WORK OF GOD as a Mother: -**
Mothers, like fathers, are indispensable in the family. In fact, the mother's love cannot be equated to anything. She keeps the family together in trying moments. Mothers are able to sense danger before it gets home. The mother has a role to play so human race can procreate and God's purpose for it could be achieved. Her duties are: -

**(i) To Evangelize**

Then leaving her water jar, the woman went back to the town and said to the people, 'Come and see a man who told me everything I ever did. Could this be the Christ?' They came out of the town and made their way toward him (John 4:28-30).

**(ii) To Help**

Then the LORD God said, 'It is not good for the man to be alone. I will make a helper suitable for him (Genesis 1:18).

**(iii) To Dedicate**

So now I give him to the LORD. For his whole life he will be given over to the LORD.' And he worshiped the LORD there (1Samuel:28).

**(iv) To Give**

She opens her arms to the poor and extends her hands to the needy (Proverbs 31:20).

In Joppa there was a disciple named Tabitha (which when translated, is Dorcas), who was always doing good and helping the poor (Acts 9:36).

**(v) To Care**

She watches over the affairs of her household and does not eat the bread of idleness (Proverbs 31:37).

When she and the members of her household were baptized, she invited us to her home. 'If you consider me a believer in the Lord,' she said, 'come and stay at my home.' And she persuaded us (Acts 16:15).

## (vi) To Submit

Wives, submit to your husbands as to the Lord. For the husband is the head of the wife as Christ is the head of the church, his body, of which he is the Savior. Now as the church submits to Christ, so also wives should submit to their husbands in everything (Ephesians 5:22- 24).

Wives, in the same way be submissive to your husbands so that, if any of any them do not believe the word, they may be won over without words by the behavior of their wives when they see they see the purity and reverence of your lives ( 1 Peter 3:1,2)

For this is the way the holy women of the past who put their hope in God used to make themselves beautiful. They were submissive to own husbands, like Sarah, who obeyed Abraham and called him her master. You are her daughters if you do what is right and do not give way to fear (1 Peter 3:5, 6).

**(c) Doing the WORK OF GOD as a Child: -**

A child's obligation, first and foremost, is to God and then to the parents. It is a fundamental duty of a child to appreciate, admire and adore the parents' contribution to his/her development; contributions that might come in many diverse ways. These are the following ways the child can reciprocate these gestures.

**(i) To Honor**

A wise son heeds the father's instruction, but a mocker does not listen to rebuke (Proverbs 13:1).

Children, obey your parents in the Lord, for this is right. 'Honor your father and mother'- which is the first commandment with a promise - 'that it may go well with you and that you may enjoy long life on the earth' (Ephesians 6:1)

**(ii) To Obey**

But Samuel replied: "Does the LORD delight in burn offerings and sacrifices as much as in obeying the voice of the LORD? To obey is better than sacrifice, to heed is better that the fat of rams (1 Samuel 15:22).

Then he went down to Nazareth with them and was obedient to them. But his mother treasured all these things in her heart. And Jesus grew in wisdom and stature, and in favor with God and men (Luke 2:51, 52).

Children, obey your parents in everything for this pleases the Lord (Colossians 3:20).

Remind the people to be subject rulers and authorities, to be obedient, to be ready to do whatever is good (Titus 3:1).

### (iii) To Care

But if a widow has children or grandchildren, these should learn first of all to put their religion into practice by caring for their own family and so repaying their parents and grandparents, for this is pleasing to God (1 Timothy 5:4).

### (iv) To Revere

Trust in the LORD with all your heart and lean not on your own understanding; in all your ways acknowledge him, and he will make your paths straight (Proverbs 3:5, 6).

The fear of the LORD teaches a man wisdom, and humility comes before honor (Proverb 15: 33).

**(v) To Listen**

My son, do forget my teaching, but keep my commands in your heart, for they will prolong your life many years and bring you prosperity. Let love and faithfulness never leave you; bind them around your neck, write them on the tablet of your heart (Proverbs 3:1-3).

My son, preserve sound judgment and discernment, do not let them out of your sight; they will be life for you, an ornament to grace your neck. Then you will go on your way in safety, and your foot will not stumble; when you lie down, you will not be afraid; when you lie down, your sleep will be sweet (Proverbs 3:21-24).

He who listens to a life-giving rebuke will be at home with the wise (Proverbs 15:31).

**(vi) To Serve**

The boy Samuel ministered before the LORD under Eli. In those days the word of the LORD was rare; there were not many visions (1 Samuel 3:1).

So he asked Jesse, 'Are these all the sons you have?' 'There is still the youngest,' Jesse answered, 'but he is tending the sheep,' Samuel said, 'Send for him, we will not sit down until he arrives' (1 Samuel 16:11).

## (2) THE WORK OF GOD IN THE CHURCH *(ALL JUDEA AND SAMARIA)*

The Church is a community of believers. These are believers who have come together after accepting Jesus Christ as the Lord and Savior. About this Christ, Paul proclaimed

> That if you confess with your mouth, "Jesus is Lord," and believe in your heart that God raised him from the dead, you will be saved. For it is with your heart that you believe and are justified, and it is with your mouth you confess and are saved (Romans 10:9, 10).

And the Church, like any living organism, must not be static but dynamic. Therefore, it must grow. And its growth could occur by the day only when the members rely on the Head, Jesus Christ. In fact, Jesus said, "…I will build my church, and the gates of Hades will not overcome it" (Matthew 16:18). Christ uses members of a church to cause the growth. That was why He warned that "…apart from me you can do nothing" (John 15:5).

Since all the members cannot do the same work, in His infinite wisdom, the Spirit has placed each member where he/she can function well. These places are **(a) the Word Ministry, (b) the Song Ministry** and **(c) the Hospitality Ministry.**

## (a) Doing the WORK OF GOD in Word Ministry as:
### (i) An Apostle

Through him and for his name's sake, we received grace and apostleship to call people from among all the Gentiles to the obedience that comes from faith (Romans 1:5).

The things that mark an apostle – signs, wonders and miracles – were done among you with great perseverance (2 Corinthians 12:12).

For God, who was at work in the ministry of Peter as an apostle to the Jews, was also at work in my ministry as an apostle to the Gentiles (Galatians 2:8).

And for this purpose I was appointed a herald and an apostle – I am not lying – am a teacher of the true faith to the Gentiles (1Timothy 2:7).

And for this gospel I was appointed a herald and an apostle and a teacher (2 Timothy 1:11).

## (ii) A Prophet

Before I formed you in the womb I knew you, before you were born I set you apart; I appointed you as a prophet to the nations (Jeremiah 1:5).

We have different gifts, according to the grace given us. If a man's gift is prophesying, let him use it in proportion to his faith (Romans 12:6).

## (iii) An Evangelist

But you, keep your head in all situations, endure hardship, do the work of an evangelist, discharge all the duties of your ministry (2 Timothy 4:5).

## (iv) A Pastor

I am the good shepherd. The good shepherd lays down his life for the sheep...I am the good shepherd; I know my sheep and my sheep know me... (John 10:11, 14).

May...our Lord Jesus, that great Shepherd of the sheep, equip you with everything good for doing his will, and may he work in us what is pleasing to him, through Jesus Christ, to whom be glory for ever and ever. Amen (Hebrews 13:20, 21).

## (v) A Teacher

Only be careful, and watch yourselves closely so that you not forget the things your eyes have seen or let them slip from your heart as long as you live. Teach them to your children and to their children after them (Deuteronomy 4:9).

As for me, far be it from me that I should sin against the LORD by failing to pray for you. And I will teach you the way that is good and right (1 Samuel 12:23).

…then hear from heaven the sin of your servants, your people Israel. Teach them the right way to live, and send rain on the land you gave your people as an inheritance (1 Kings 8:36).

He will teach us his ways, so that we may walk in his path. The law will go out from Zion, the word of the LORD from Jerusalem (Micah 4:2).

You must teach what is in accord with sound doctrine, teach the older men to be temperate, worthy of respect, self-controlled, and sound in faith, in love and in endurance. Likewise, teach the older women to be reverent in the way they live, not to be slanderers or addicted to much wine, but to teach what is good (Titus 2:1-3).

## (b) Doing the WORK OF GOD in Song Ministry through: -
### (i) Worship

Ascribe to the LORD. O families of nations, ascribe to the LORD glory and strength, ascribe to the LORD glory due his name, Bring an offering and come before him; worship the in the splendor of his holiness ( 1 Chronicles 16:28, 29).

Come, let us bow down in worship, let us kneel before the LORD our Maker; for he is our God and we are the people of his pasture, the flock under his care (Psalm 95:6, 7).
Shout for joy to the LORD, all earth. Worship the LORD with gladness; come before with joyful songs (Psalm 100:1, 2).

### (ii) Praises

I will proclaim the name of the LORD. Oh, praise the greatness of our God! He is the rock, his works are perfect, and all his ways are just. A faithful God who does no wrong, upright and just is he (Deuteronomy 32:3, 4).

...Praise be to you, O LORD, God of our father Israel, from everlasting to everlasting. Yours, O LORD, is the greatness and the power and the glory and the majesty and the splendor, for everything in heaven and earth is yours. Yours, O LORD, is the kingdom; you are exalted as head over all (1 Chronicles 29:10, 11).

I will praise you, O LORD, with all my heart; I will tell of all your wonders. I will be glad and rejoice I you; I will sing praise to your name, O Most High (Psalm 9:1, 2).

I will praise the LORD who counsels me; even at night my heart instructs me. I have set the LORD always before me. Because he is at my right hand, I will not be shaken (Psalm 16: 7, 8).

Sing to the LORD a new song; sing to the LORD, all the earth. Sing to the LORD, praise his name; proclaim his salvation day after day (Psalm 96:1, 2).

Sing to him, sing praise to him; tell of all his wonderful acts (Psalm 105:2).

## (iii) Dancing

David, wearing a linen ephod, danced before the LORD with all his might, while he and the entire house of Israel brought up the ark of the LORD with shouts and the sound of trumpets (2 Samuel 6:14).

Let Israel rejoice in their Maker, let the people of Zion be glad in their King. Let them praise his name with dancing and make music to him with tambourine and harp (Psalm 149:2, 3).

## (iv) Instruments

Praise him with the sounding of the trumpet, praise him with the harp and lyre, praise him with tambourine and dancing, praise him with the strings and flute, praise him with the clash of cymbals, praise him with resounding cymbals (Psalms 150:3-5).

## (c) Doing the WORK OF GOD in Hospitality Ministry through: -

### (i) Service

Serve the LORD with fear and rejoice with trembling (Psalm 2:11).

the Son of Man did not come to be served, but to serve, and give his life as a ransom for many (Matthew 20:28).

You, my brothers, were called to be free. But do not use your freedom to indulge the sinful nature; rather, serve one another in love (Galatians 5:13).
Serve wholeheartedly, as if you were serving the Lord, not men (Ephesians 6:7).

Each one should use whatever gift he has received to serve others, faithfully administering God's grace in its various form (1 Peter 4:10).

### (ii) Visitation

For I was hungry and you gave me something to eat, I was thirsty and you gave me something to drink…I needed clothes and you clothed me, I was sick and you looked after me, I was in prison and you came to visit me (Matthew 25:35, 36).

But you, O God, do see trouble and grief; you consider it to take it in hand. The victim commits himself to you; you are the helper of the fatherless (Psalm 10:14).

In Joppa there was a disciple named Tabitha (which when translated, is Dorcas), who was always doing good and helping the poor (Acts 9:36).

## (iii) Assistance

If it is serving, let him serve; if it is encouraging, let him encourage; if it is contributing to the needs of others, let him give generously; if it is leadership, let him govern diligently; if it is showing mercy, let him do it cheerfully (Roman 12:7, 8).

and well known for her good deeds, such as bringing up children, showing hospitality, washing the feet of the saints, helping those in trouble and devoting herself to all kind of good deeds (1 Timothy 5:10).

## (iv) Cleaning

After that, he poured water into a basin and began to wash his disciples' feet, drying them with the towel wrapped around his waist (John 13:5).

## (3) THE WORK OF GOD IN THE COMMUNITY (THE ENDS OF THE EARTH)

The believer owes the community a duty as a Christian, just as he or she does the family and the church. In fact, where the family and the church's boundaries end, that of the community immediately begins from there. With the community aware of the duty a believer owes it, it had set standards for the believer to meet. And these standards couldn't be higher as far as our responsibilities are concerned. The community watches our moves and ways. But irrespective of this scrutiny from the community, the believer is called to live above it, influence it and make a difference. The believer cannot afford to exempt himself/herself from interacting with the people from outside the immediate family and the church. Our presence must be felt. We are called to be "the salt of the earth" and "light of the world" (Matthew 5:13, 14). We are in the community to win it for Christ. Knowing that, Jesus made it exquisitely clear when He counseled that,

> In this same way, let your light shine before men that they may see your good deeds and praise your Father in heaven (Matthew 5:16).

To effectively continue with the mandate given so as to make a difference in the community, Jesus assured the disciples that the authority they would need has been given to Him (Matthew 28:18). Depending upon this powerful position He had acquired, He requested them, and us, as believers to

> ...go and make disciples of all nations, baptizing them in the name of the Father, and of the Son and of the Holy Spirit, and teaching them to obey everything I

have commanded you. And surely I am with you to the end of age (Matthew 28:19, 20).

But the fundamental question posed to the believer is "...how can they preach if they are not sent?" Our presence completely answers that question. It is written, 'How beautiful are the feet of those who bring good news!" (Romans 10:15). With this assurance in our hearts, we have the following to fulfill in the community - **(a) Spiritual Obligation, (b) Civil Obligation, (c) Moral Obligation** and **(d) Social Obligation.**

### (a) Doing the WORK OF GOD in the Community as a Spiritual Obligation:-

(i) <u>Salt</u>

You are the salt of the earth. But if the salt loses its saltines, how can it be made salty again? It is no longer good for anything except to be thrown out and trampled by men (Matthew 5:13).

(ii) <u>Light</u>

You are the light of the world. A city on a hill cannot be hidden. Neither do people light a lamp and put it under a bowl. Instead, they put it on its stand, and it gives light to everyone in the house (Matthew 5:14).

### (iii) Transformation

Do not conform any longer to the pattern of this world, but be transformed by the renewing of your mind, Then you will be able to test and approve what God's will is – his good, pleasing and perfect will (Romans 12:2).

### (iv) Leadership

Give me wisdom and knowledge, that I may lead this people, for who is able to govern this great people of yours? (2 Chronicles 1:10).

He makes me lie down in green pastures, he leads me beside quiet waters, he restores my soul (Psalm 23:2).

The watchman opens the gate for him, and the sheep listen to his voice. He calls his own sheep by name and leads them out (John 10:3).

## (b) Doing the WORK OF GOD in the Community as a Civil Obligation: -

### (i) Taxation

Show me the coin used for paying tax." They brought him a denarius, and he asked them, "Whose portrait is this? 'Caesar's,' they replied. Then he said to them,

'Give to Caesar what is Caesar's, and to God what is God's' (Matthew 22:21).

Give everyone what you owe him: if you owe taxes, pay taxes; if revenue, then revenue; if respect, then respect; if honor, then honor (Romans 13:7).

(ii) <u>Submission</u>

Everyone must submit himself to the governing authorities, for there is no authority except that which God has established. The authorities that exist have been established by God...

For rulers hold no terror for those who do right, but for those who do wrong. Do you want to be free from fear of the one in authority? Then do what is right and he will commend you...

Therefore, it is necessary to submit to the authorities, not only because of possible punishment but also because of conscience (Roman 1:1, 3, 5).
Remind the people to be subject to rulers and authorities, to be obedient, to be ready to do whatever is good (Titus 3:1).

## (c) Doing the WORK OF GOD in the Community as a Moral Obligation: -

### (i) Peace

He will proclaim peace to the nations. His rule will extend from sea to sea and from the River to the ends of the earth (Zechariah 9:10).

Salt is good, but if it loses its saltiness, how can you make it salty again? Have salt in yourselves, and be at peace with each other (Mark 9:50).

Peacemakers who sow in peace raise a harvest of righteousness (James 3:18).

To slander no one, to be peaceable and considerate, and to show humility toward all men (Titus 3:2).

### (ii) Generosity

Cast your bread upon the waters, for after many days you will find it again. Give portion to seven, yes to eight, for you do not know what disaster may come upon the land (Ecclesiastes 11:1,2).

But when you give to the needy, do not let left hand know what your right hand is doing, so that your giving may be in secret. Then your Father, who sees what is done in secret, will reward you (Matthew 6:3, 4).

Give, and it will be given to you. A good measure, pressed down, shaken together and running over, will be poured into your lap. For whatever measure you use, it will be measured to you (Mark 6:38).

Let no debt remain outstanding, except the continuing debt to love one another, for he who loves his fellowman has fulfilled the law' (Romans 13:8).

Remember this: Whoever sows sparingly will reap sparingly, and whoever sows generously will also reap generously. Each man should give what he has decided in his heart to give, not reluctantly or under compulsion, for God loves a cheerful giver (2 Corinthians 9:6, 7).

### (d) Doing the WORK OF GOD in the Community as a Social Obligation: -

### (i) Separation

Blessed is the man who does not walk in the counsel of the wicked or stand in the way of sinners or sit in the seat of mockers (Psalm 1:1).

Turn from evil and do good; seek peace and pursue it (Psalm 34:14).

## (i) Pleasing

The man with integrity walks securely, but he who takes crooked paths will be found out (Proverbs 10:9).

When a man's ways are pleasing to the LORD, he makes his enemies live at peace with him (Proverbs 16:7).

## (ii) Humility

Before his downfall a man's heart is proud, but humility comes before honor (Proverbs 18:12).
Humility and fear of the LORD bring wealth and honor and life (Proverb 22:4).

## (iii) Holiness

But his delight is in the law of the LORD, and on his law he meditates day and night (Psalm 1:2).

Drink water from your own cistern, running water from your own well (Proverbs 5:15).

Make every effort to live in peace with all men and to be holy; without holiness no one will see the Lord (Hebrews 12:14).

At this juncture, we bring down the curtains regarding what the WORK OF GOD is. It is so fascinating to note that its definition and content go beyond the walls of a church building. In the following pages, we will make the attempt to compare the two; the WORD OF GOD verses the WORK OF GOD. We're making this comparison in order to find out the difference between them; that is if there is any at all.

# THREE

## What Is the Difference?

*"Your <u>WORD</u> is a lamp to my feet and a light for my path"* (Psalm 119:105).

Having considered what the WORD OF GOD and the WORK OF GOD are, we will proceed to find out if there is any difference between them. I believe the line between them is so thin, if care is not taken, we might end up bundling them into one box. The Bible is still the best source from which we can glean such knowledge. It is thoroughly imbued with so many instances we can consider. But we will tackle just a few in this attempt.

The sun was directly over their heads. The sky above was crystal clear that particular afternoon. This cloudless sky caused the sun to have a field day. It pummeled its victims with its summer biting heat. Everyone was sweating profusely though they were resting under this big tree. After He wiped the beads of sweat running down His humble face, Jesus turned to Peter and asked him what the time was. Peter answered politely, but never bothered to look at Jesus' face. But thereafter, he took advantage of the broken silence to remind Jesus He had promised to visit Lazarus' sisters. "Oh yes! Is it today?" Jesus shot back rhetorically. Matthew was sitting close to Him at this time so he responded devoid of any hesitation. "Yes today. Have you forgotten, Teacher?" he enquired aggressively. But there was no response from Jesus.

Jesus cleared His throat. Then slowly, He laid His head on the small rock lying behind Him as if He did not care about the promise He'd made to the sisters. Absolute silence prevailed. The Apostles turned to look at each other's face. They were surprised at His attitude, yet no one dared to ask a question. Jesus ceased this silent moment to catch a short rest for His tired body. In no time, the few seconds they were courting gave way to minutes and hours. When He had finished the short snap, He ordered them to get ready for the visit as He had promised. "What manner of Man is this? A Man whose next move you cannot predict" the Apostles thought of Him.

## What is the difference?

They gathered around Jesus before leaving for Bethany. When they had walked, with a few miles away from their hosts, they scattered. They walked in pairs as if someone had insisted on that idea. Some folks recognized them so they followed. In no time, words had reached Lazarus' sisters. They were informed Jesus and His disciples were heading in their direction. Martha and Mary knew He would not pass by without spending some time in their abode. As usual, Martha began to do what she knew how to do best. She was putting pieces together in the kitchen to prepare some meals for them.

"Lazarus, Lazarus," she called at the pitch of her voice in an attempt to locate him. Lazarus was then in the stall attending to the sheep and the goats. He was informed by a friend of his sister's call. He immediately left everything and attended to her.

"Lazarus, I heard the Teacher and His Apostles are coming here, and we must prepare something for them," Martha informed Lazarus without patiently waiting for him to get nearer. She went on to request him to fetch a few items for her. Martha was in the middle of issuing her directives when Jesus and the Apostles entered their fenced compound. They had a crowd of people tailing after them. Mary was in her room. But when she heard of the commotion on their compound, she dashed out at a lightning speed. She awkwardly drew nearer to the Teacher and shyly exchanged the customary greetings with them. Then, she pointed to the seats made ready for them. Humbly, she requested them to make themselves comfortable and feel at home. They accepted her courteous gesture and reclined under that canopy-shaped tree. They were enjoying the fresh air. A little girl from the next house climbed on to Jesus' lap. One of the Apostles wanted to prevent her. But He grabbed this opportunity to teach them another lesson.

> When Jesus saw this, he was indignant. He said to them, "Let the children come to me, and do not hinder them, for the kingdom of God belongs to such as these. I tell you the truth, anyone who will not receive the kingdom of God like a little child will never enter it (Mark 10:14, 15).

Jesus' words had not ceased falling from His lips when Martha dashed out of the kitchen sweating profusely. She approached Jesus with her concern. Luke described this captivating scene in these words.

> But Martha was distracted by all the preparations that had to be made. She came to him and asked, 'Lord, don't you care that my sister has left me to do the work by myself? Tell her to help me.' (Luke 10:40).

The eloquence with which Jesus churned His words arrested Mary's attention and she pinned it to His direction. She never considered joining her elder sister in the kitchen. As a matter of fact, it never occurred to her to give that a consideration. Then Jesus humbly looked Martha's way and regarded her. He pitied her too. Martha never recognized that her request was out of step. Jesus pulled Himself together and considered the presence of the crowd. But He could not shy away from the truth. So slowly, He lifted His head up and looked straight into her eyes. Then, as captured by Luke, in a soft tone let this caution out:

> "Martha, Martha," the Lord answered, "you are worried and upset about many things, but only one thing is needed. Mary has chosen what is better, and it will not be taken away from her" (Luke 10:41, 42).

Jesus' answer sent Martha into a state of dilemma. She was shocked and confused. *"Does He really care as He had made us to know that He does? Doesn't He understand what I mean? And if He does, why should He reprimand me?"* These and many other questions flooded her mind. Yet she could not make any head and tail out of it. Here is the clash of the WORD OF GOD and the WORK OF GOD. Was Martha right or not when she demanded assistance from her sister? One might think that Jesus was downplaying the importance of the

WORK. Not so at all. The work a believer does for the Lord is the outward manifestation of one's inward faith. This is the way James declared it;

> But someone will say, 'You have faith; I have deeds.' Show me your faith without deeds, and I will show you my faith by what I do (James 2:18).

"Then why did He respond to Martha with such a statement?" someone might ask. Jesus wanted Martha to know that the two - the WORD OF GOD and the WORK OF GOD - are not the same and, not even similar. Preparing food for Jesus and His apostles is a privilege in a life time. And therefore, its importance should never be consigned to the background. But the WORD OF GOD cannot be listened to and the WORK OF GOD be done at the same time. One must take precedence over the other when they happen to clash at a particular time. That was the truth Jesus wanted to convey.

Apostle Paul proved the difference between the WORD OF GOD and the WORK OF GOD when he was writing to the recipients of his Ephesians' letter. There is the probability an issue similar to that of Martha and Mary's might have cropped up in the church. And that might have resulted in strong divisions among the believers. So, being the founder of the church, his counsel was immediately sought to help put the issue to rest, as well as to restore unity. Like every good leader, Paul put himself to work to bring about this much-sought unity. Then he responded saying,

> For it is by grace you have been saved through faith - and this not from yourselves, it is a gift from God - not by works so that no one can boast (Ephesians 2:8, 9).

Paul, without any intimidation, made the preeminence of the WORD OF GOD plainly. He clearly pointed out that "You have been saved through faith…" which came about "from hearing the message, (the WORD OF GOD)" and "not by works (the WORK OF GOD) so that no one can boast" (Ephesians2:8; Romans 10:17; Ephesians 2:9).

Peter came along with his effort to complement Paul's argument. The lifestyle of those Peter was writing to might have been questionable. So he took this privilege to address them. Since some of them might have come from pagan background, holiness was difficult a task to be adhered to. Peter wrote to caution them, from which he drew the difference between the WORD OF GOD and the WORK OF GOD. In fact, he stated categorically that,

> For you have been born again, not of perishable seed, but of imperishable, through the living and enduring WORD OF GOD (1 Peter 1:23).

He made them to be aware of the price paid to redeem the believer. It is so high that, they cannot afford to tarnish its reputation. In fact, he wanted to make it crystal clear that they were born again, not by the WORK OF GOD they did but, through the WORD OF GOD they heard. It's through the WORD OF GOD when one hears it that the Holy Spirit convicts for a change in one's life and one's heart. Luke recorded in Acts the effect of Peter's powerful message on the day of Pentecost. He said,

> When the people heard this (the WORD OF GOD), they were cut to the heart and said to Peter and the other apostles, 'Brothers, what shall we do?' (Acts 2:37).

It does not matter the number of hours one spends in doing the WORK OF GOD, it won't "set you free" apart from the WORD OF GOD. In the course of discharging our duties as Christians, there will be temptations along the way. There would be mountains to be scaled and valleys to come out from. In fact, Jesus did not shy away from this plain truth. He turned and said to the disciples,

I have told you these things, so that in me you may have peace. In this world you will have trouble. But take heart! I have overcome the world (John 16:33).

When one decides to do the WORK OF GOD, there would be decisions to be taken at crossroads and confusions to be overcome. For that matter, David counseled, saying, "Your WORD is a lamp to my feet and a light for my path" (Psalm 119:105). This "lamp" helps the believer navigate through this good life we're gifted with. He went further to let us know the WORD will also protect us from falling into Satan's trap. "I have hidden your WORD in my heart that I might not sin against you," he concluded (Psalm 119:11).

It is not the WORK OF GOD one does that transforms one's life. Instead, it is the WORD OF GOD. By its power, it encourages, inspires, impels, prompts and cheers one on to effectively do the WORK OF GOD. It inflates one's commitment and courage, one's dedication and determination so that one would not shy away from the WORK but eagerly persevere in doing it. There are problems associated with the WORK OF GOD. If one doesn't know the WORD OF GOD enough from which to draw confidence, encouragement and strength, one would easily give up.

The Word of God vs. the Work of God

The recipients of the Hebrews letter might be Jewish Christians but residing outside the Jewish land. The content revealed that these Christians were undergoing terrible persecutions. The writer might have had an acquaintance with them. He decided to script these few words as a way of lifting their spirits up. So in this said letter, he elevated the difference between the WORD OF GOD and the WORK OF GOD by saying;

> For the WORD OF GOD is living and active. Sharper than any double-edged sword, it penetrates even to the dividing soul and spirit, joints and marrow; it judges the thoughts and attitudes of the heart (Hebrews 4:12).

The letter to the Hebrews from the verse above, described the WORD OF GOD to the recipients in these five ways: -

(a) **It's Living**

> The WORD became flesh and made his dwelling among us. We have seen his glory, the glory of the One and Only, who came from the Father, full of grace and truth (John 1:14).

(b) **It's Active**
> Then he said to me, "Prophecy to these bones and say hear the WORD of the LORD! This is what the

Sovereign LORD says to these bones: I will make breath to enter you, and you will come to life. I will attach tendons to you and make flesh come upon you and cover you with skin; I will put breath in you, and you will come to life. Then you will know that I am the LORD" (Ezekiel 37:4, 5).

### (c) It's Sharper

When the people heard this, they were cut to the heart and said to Peter and the other apostles, "Brothers, what shall we do?" (Acts 2:37).

### (d) It Penetrates

In him was life, and that life was the light of men. The light shines in the darkness, but the darkness has not understood it. The true light that gives light to every man was coming into the world (John 1:4,5,9).

### (e) It Judges

Let the heaven rejoice, let the earth be glad; let the sea resound, and all that is in it; let the fields be jubilant, and everything in them. Then all the trees of the forest will sing for joy; they will sing before the LORD, for he comes, he comes to judge the earth. He will judge in righteousness and the peoples in his truth (Psalm 96:11-13).

These five characteristics of the WORD OF GOD, as shown by the letter's author, cannot be attributed to the WORK OF GOD. The WORK OF GOD cannot live and be active without human involvement. It is not sharper, neither does it penetrate nor judges a person. This therefore authenticates, as well as boosts the arguments related to this difference indicated earlier on.

On two other occasions, Jesus again ascertained this fact of the WORD OF GOD's importance. On one occasion, the Pharisees had a confrontation with Him, when He claimed that, "I am the light of the world. Whoever follows me will never walk in darkness, but will have the light of life" (John 8:12). Those Pharisees were indignant of His claim. They accused Him of validating His own testimony. But His argument was persuasive. As a result, a few Jews among the Pharisees believed. Jesus ceased the opportunity and explained the importance of the WORD OF GOD as compared to the WORK OF GOD. He said, "…you will know the truth (WORD OF GOD), and the truth will set you free (John 8:32). The WORK OF GOD does not and cannot set one free from the falsehood being peddled around in our time.

## What is the difference?

On the other, when in an isolated place with the Apostles just before He went to the cross, He went further to decipher the truth. He trumpeted to them that "…If you remain in me and my words (WORD OF GOD) remain in you, ask whatever you wish and it will be given you" (John 15:7). At this juncture, He showed once again the difference between the two: the WORD OF GOD and the WORK OF GOD. He emphatically insisted on the WORD OF GOD, which when it remains in one's life, whatever one would ask, would be granted so glory will come to the Father.

# FOUR

## What Is the Relationship?

*As the rain and the snow come down from heaven, and do not return to it without watering the earth and making it bud and flourish, so that it yields seed for the sower and bread for the eater, so is my <u>WORD</u> that goes out of my mouth: It will not return to me empty, but will accomplish what I desire and achieve the purpose for which I sent it* (Isaiah 55:10, 11).

Though there is a vast difference between the WORD OF GOD and the WORK OF GOD, amazingly, they are closely related. The Bible has revealed this fascinating phenomenon and it couldn't have proven this relationship better. It is so much sobering when one realizes this truth. And this knowledge of the truth will tend to reduce one's level of anxiety when one happens to be faced with a choice at a particular time: to listen to the WORD OF GOD or just go and do the WORK OF GOD. Honestly speaking, the WORK OF GOD has its curves, twists and turns. That's to say, the WORK OF GOD has its own sets of problems. However, there is a fundamental truth associated with this assertion. That the outcome - or simply put, the success of the WORK OF GOD - depends on the WORD OF GOD and how richly it dwells in the one carrying out the WORK. How much time one spends reading, studying, and knowing the WORD OF GOD, coupled with meditation, prayers and fasting, will determine the outcome of the WORK OF GOD one is called upon to do.

In five laborious days, the LORD created the heaven and earth, and everything that is in it. The birds of the air, the fishes of the sea and animals that walk the land, He called into being. He fashioned plants for food and medicinal purposes (Psalm 24:1, 2). On the sixth day, the LORD created man. He put him in the garden to take care of it. Man was permitted to touch and use everything but one, the tree; the tree of knowledge of good and evil.

> The LORD God took the man and put him in the Garden of Eden to work it and take care of it. And the LORD God commanded the man, "You are free

to eat from any tree in the garden, but you must not eat from the tree of knowledge of good and evil, for when you eat of it you will surely die" (Genesis 2:15-17).

Man's successful stay in the Garden depended on his adherence to the command (WORD OF GOD) the LORD issued. But man could not obey the commands of the LORD.

This disobedience set humanity on a collision course with itself. The search for a fulfillment in life had since eluded mankind for generations, one after another. It was in the midst of this search that the children of God found themselves in Egypt, where they had been slaves for about four hundred and thirty years. Out of their cry for deliverance, the LORD prepared Moses to lead them from this bondage. He led them to the edge of the Promised Land. They were going into a land that was flowing with milk and honey. A land the LORD had promised to give their ancestors but was inhabited by heathen inhabitants. Like every good leader, Moses assembled them for a last-minute talk. He appealed that

> If you fully obey the LORD your God and carefully follow all his command (WORD OF GOD) I give you today, the LORD your God will set you high

above all the nations on earth. All these blessings will come upon you and accompany you if you obey the LORD your God (Deuteronomy 28:1, 2).

The blessings God's people were going to accrue and enjoy would be determined by their obedience to the LORD's command (the WORD OF GOD).

From a burning bush, the LORD called and outlined all that was to be done. Moses was tending a herd of sheep for Jethro, his father-in-law, the priest of Midian. Moses was mandated to lead the Israelites from Egypt where they were being held captives for the past four hundred years and more. A task so intense and mighty in his eyes, he employed all possible means to escape but to no avail. From God's perspective, there was no one better prepared than Moses. For every excuse he churned out, the LORD had another option on the table. He was not able to outwit God with his excuses. The children of God were to use the wilderness as their passage way to the Promised Land. Moses had walked this terrain for forty years. He was the one aptly equipped to carry out this monumental operation. For the period following their first interaction, Moses humbly followed the LORD's statutes and commands. Unfortunately, he refused to obey a command from God when they were just about to cross over to the Promised Land. He was therefore barred from being part of what had been promised their forefathers. Someone else must execute the job.

In this same way, the LORD extended the same appeal to Joshua when he was going to take the mantle from his predecessor, Moses. The LORD soon chose Joshua to carry on with the mantle from where Moses had left it. He felt overwrought when he was informed with the news. Having worked alongside Moses, and had seen the miracle the LORD performed through him, he felt he could not fit into Moses' 'shoes.' God knew and therefore assured him saying; "Be strong and courageous, because you will lead these people into the land I swore to their forefathers to give to them" (Joshua 1:6). The journey to the Promised Land, though so significant, it was not as it was to dwell among the Gentiles. For this reason, the LORD would have to caution Joshua. He said,

> Do not let this Book of the Law of the LORD depart from your mouth, meditate on it day and night, SO that you may be careful to do everything written in it. Then you will be prosperous and successful (Joshua 1:8).

Three precautionary measures the LORD required of Joshua and his followers to be carried out in the Promised Land regarding the WORD OF GOD. They were: -

(a) Do not let it depart from your mouth,
(b) Do meditate on it day and night,
(c) Do everything written in it.

Joshua and his people were not going to fold their arms and expect manna to rain from heaven like it did while they were in the wilderness. They must surely venture into some endeavors of life: religious, social and moral. In the course of discharging their duties, they would need to be guided by a code of conduct. This is where the WORD OF GOD transpired. And the three particular measures above were what the LORD required of them. If they would adhere strictly to them, prosperity and success will then be theirs in the land.

Like Joshua - receiving instructions from the LORD as to how they would conduct themselves in the Promised Land - so was Solomon from his father David. Solomon was promised to be the builder of the temple (2 Samuel 7: 12). David knew the stakes could not be higher. Then he recalled the oath the LORD swore to him.

> The LORD swore an oath to David, a sure oath that he will not revoke: "One of your own descendants I will place on your throne - if your sons keep my covenant and the statutes I teach them, then their

## What is the relationship?

sons will sit on your throne forever and ever" (Psalm 132:11,12).

So when David was about to go the way of his ancestors he called Solomon, the heir apparent, into his presence. David established how faithful the LORD was with him when he obeyed His commandments, as well as the benefits he accrued. From this wonderful experience, David cautioned his son to walk with Him in the same manner.

> "I am about to go the way of all the earth" he said. "So be strong, show yourself a man, and observe what the LORD your God requires: Walk in his ways, and keep his decrees and commands, his laws and requirements, as written in the Law of Moses, so that you may prosper in all you do and wherever you go and that the LORD may keep his promise to me: 'If your descendants watch how they live, and if they walk faithfully before me with all their heart and soul, you will never fail to have a man on the throne of Israel' (1Kings 2: 2-4).

The task of leading this rebellious nation was enormous and daunting. This is a rebellious group of people. Their hearts were hardened. This task of leading this nation - a nation that rebelled against the LORD in many instances - demands astounding confidence and immense courage. It also calls for a supernatural power and a special ability to succeed. These attributes would propel such a leader to each and every height. David expected Solomon to demonstrate these qualities. But to the father's surprise, these qualities were to no avail when he called for his enthronement. These attributes were lacking in his son's life after all. David knew immediately Solomon was vulnerable. David had been a victim to such temptations associated with these kinds of positions: especially when one is endowed with absolute power analogous to the king of Israel.

David led Israel for about forty years. And this was the period the kingdom of Israel experienced the most peaceful atmosphere. Yet, this peaceful kingdom was not free from its own version of controversies and myriads of problems (1 Samuel Chapters 11 & 12). As this rugged life of ours attempts to consume our endeavors, every leader like Solomon, needs substantial amount of information from a skillful or wise person to help him navigate through any adventure. The father had enough amount of this skill. And from that rich experience rooted in innate wisdom and faith, David sounded a strong note of warning to his son. He ambiguously emphasized the principles he should stick to. And this is what he said to him:

...Walk in his ways, and keep his decrees and commands, his laws and requirements (WORD OF GOD), as written in the Law of Moses, <u>SO</u> that you may prosper in all you do and wherever you go (1 Kings 2:3).

When the time was fully due, Solomon was installed as David's successor. The ceremony culminating in the succession happened just as David instructed the priest and the prophet to do. In a short span of time after the succession ceremony, David passed away to join his ancestors. Solomon had begun his reign and had secured the throne. Then a visitation from the LORD occurred. The omniscient LORD, knowing how much Solomon would besmirch his position as the king of Israel, descended to caution him to

> walk in my ways and obey my statutes and commands (WORD OF GOD) as David your father did, [and] I will give you long life (1Kings 3:14).

Solomon had come of age now. And surely, he did soil the image of God through disobedience. Solomon pursued foreign women; the very path he was cautioned not to walk. He violated the LORD's statutes and switched his faithful allegiance from God to his own self-seeking pleasures. Solomon ended up bowing down to graven images and lifeless idols fashioned from wood by human hands. The very things he was warned to desist from, he indulged in without any reservations. At the end of the day, he coveted the wrath of God.

> The LORD became angry with Solomon because his heart had turned away from the LORD, the God of Israel, who had appeared to him twice. Although he had forbidden Solomon to follow other gods, Solomon did not keep the LORD's command. So the LORD said to Solomon, "Since this is your attitude and you have not kept my covenant and my decrees, which I commanded you, I will most certainly tear the kingdom away from you and give it to one of your subordinates (1Kings 11:9-11).

Despite the prosperous experience he acquired from leading the kingdom of Israel and the chaos he caused for himself, he dispensed this wisdom to his son. Solomon learned a simple lesson the hard way; he could do nothing apart from God. So when Solomon had called his son into his presence, he also advised him saying;

> My son, do not forget my teaching, but keep my commands (WORD OF GOD) in your heart, for they will prolong your life many years and bring you prosperity (Proverbs 3:1,2).

## What is the relationship?

In the New Testament, one significant example of the early believers was when a dispute ensued between the Grecian Jews and their Hebraic brethren. This issue concerned the daily food distributions. The Grecian widows were being overlooked. Then the Grecians Jews raised their concerns (Acts 6:1). Possibly, the leaders might have been doing everything; leading in prayers, sharing the food, etc. This incident exposed the weakness in their management style. But out of it, Peter learned something. To daily arbitrate and resolve this conflict will consume much of the disciples' time. Yet the incident must be resolved, or be contained, to put it mildly. When Peter realized his shortcomings, he sought a perfect and permanent solution that would appease both parties. He realized that the Christian journey is not engaged in a democratic manner (government by the people) but theocratic (government by God), where God is the one who ordains and rules. This journey, Peter also realized, is not only physical, but spiritual too. So Peter sought the face of God. After spending some time in His presence, Peter suggested to his fellow disciples thus:

> ...It would not be right for us to neglect the ministry of the WORD OF GOD in order to wait on tables. Brothers, choose seven men from among you who are known to be full of the Spirit and wisdom. We will turn this responsibility (WORK OF GOD) over to

them and we will give our attention to prayer and the ministry of the WORD (Acts 6:2-4).

Peter distinctly separated the WORD OF GOD from the WORK OF GOD. And he assigned the WORK to the people "who are known to be full of the Spirit and wisdom." He could have held on to the responsibility of leading and giving directives here and there. After all, he was the leader, and such an enviable position should have inflated his ego. Yet, he allowed the success of the WORK OF GOD to supersede his personal interests.

It is unfortunate some men of God fall victim to grappling with all the WORK OF GOD. They refuse to delegate others to assist them. Instead of spending enough time to study the WORD OF GOD, they would rather choose to hold on tight to the WORK OF GOD as if someone is at their heels to take it away. These men of God fail to realize that when others are delegated, it would leave them with enough time to be in the presence of God. And in addition, the work would be effectively carried out to its successful end too. A pastor friend, Rev. George Abaidoo summed up their attitudes this way: "They are so much going after the WORK OF GOD that they barely have enough time to go after the GOD of the WORK." Jesus humbly appealed to

## What is the relationship?

His Apostles to rely on Him and His teachings for "apart from me you can do nothing" (John 15:5).

Paul observed the relationship between the WORD OF GOD and the WORK OF GOD when he was writing his second letter to Timothy. Timothy, the young pastor whom Paul recognized as a faithful man and mentored, was receiving a missive of encouragement from his mentor. Paul realized his spiritual son's timidity. There was no other way to prop him up but to emphasize the essence of the WORD OF GOD as related to the WORK OF GOD. He said,

> All scripture (WORD OF GOD) is God-breathed and is useful for teaching (WORK OF GOD) in righteousness so that the man of God may be thoroughly equipped for every good work (2Timothy 3:6).

Paul used the words, "and is useful for," to project their relationship so that the worker "may be thoroughly equipped for every good work" that he might come across as he pursues his calling.

# FIVE

## What Is the Observation?

*"If you remain in me and my <u>WORDS</u> remain in you, ask whatever you wish, and it will be given you" (John 15:7).*

On the previous pages, we identified the WORD OF GOD and the WORK OF GOD. We went on to find how different and yet, how related they are. And having considered their characteristics - from which we realized how different, yet how related they are - we will lastly draw observation from the analyses we compiled. To achieve this, we have to consider the various powerful men of the Bible. Their lives embodied the most vivid answers to the question: 'what is the observation?'

The prophet Samuel anointed Saul as the first king over Israel. The Israelites forced God to bend His hands when they demanded a king like the other nations. They would want their future king to lead them to wars as the other surrounding nations were doing. Though this demand for a king was an indictment on God's compassion, grace and love He had towards His people, He went on to meet their request with a broken heart. Nevertheless, He was with them since whatever His promises to do, He never fails to.

One day, Samuel asked the king, Saul, to

> Go down ahead of me to Gilgal. I will surely come down to you to sacrifice burnt offerings and fellowship offerings, but you must wait seven days until I come to tell what you are to do (1 Samuel 10:8).

Saul did just as prophet Samuel requested him to do. However, in the course of waiting, there were threats from the Philistines who had laid siege. The Philistine camp was comprised of three thousand chariots, six thousand charioteers, and foot soldiers as numerous as the sand on the seashore. This heavy presence of equipment and fighters sent shuddering and trembling throughout the camp of the Israelites. This information reached the king, Saul, who was overtaken and gripped with fear. So immediately, he assembled nearly three thousand men from Israel while he waited for Prophet Samuel's arrival. He had the patience to wait for the seven days. And when the prophet did not show up at the time he expected him, King Saul couldn't gather enough guts to wait any further. King Saul decided to take the place of Prophet Samuel. He went ahead and sacrificed the burnt and fellowship offerings. Just as he had finished, Samuel finally arrived.

Saul went and greeted Samuel. Saul did not suspect Samuel's awareness of the sacrifice he offered. The prophet knew immediately something was amiss. The Spirit revealed it to Prophet Samuel that Saul did sacrifice so the prophet questioned him thus:

> "What have you done?" asked Samuel. Saul replied, "When I saw that the men were scattering, and that you did not come at the set time, and that the Philistines were assembling at Micmash, I thought 'Now the Philistines will come down against me at Gilgal, and I have not sought the LORD's favor.' So I felt compelled to offer the burnt offering" (1 Samuel 13, 11, 12).

Saul's answer shocked the man of God. He flew into rage as a result. Samuel was highly offended by this gross disobedience. He did not hesitate to draw Saul's attention to this foolish act of his. He rebuked him thus;

"You acted foolishly," Samuel said. "You have not kept the command (the WORD OF GOD) the LORD your God gave you; if you had, he would have established your kingdom (WORK OF GOD) over Israel all time" (1Samuel 13:13).

Saul stood there stunned to the core of his being. His demeanor disclosed the intensity of his predicament. Samuel repeated to Saul, "Yes, 'You acted foolishly,'" to reiterate his objection to Saul's conduct. Patience is a virtue. In fact, it is fruit of the Spirit. Therefore, it's cultivated not by one's own effort but, by the power of the Holy Spirit (Galatians 5:22). Solomon, knowing so well from his personal experience, advised that "Better a patient man than a warrior..." (Proverbs 16:32). Why couldn't Saul show such virtue at the time when it was most needed? Why wasn't Saul able to just obey the prophet's instructions? Why didn't he realize he was not the one designated to perform such sacrifices? The answer was simple! Saul never took the WORD OF GOD seriously all the while. For this reason, he could not nurture the virtue of patience. He never developed strong relationship with God through His WORDS. The king was more obsessed with the WORK OF GOD than he was with the WORD OF GOD. "Your WORD is a lamp to my feet and a light for my path," David observed (Psalm 119:105). Saul never comprehended that, even though he saw David

## What is the Observation?

walked the corridors of his palace for many years. Pleasing his subjects to claim applause and vain glory was all that mattered to him. Why? So his (Saul's) name could be lifted high. Pleasing the LORD was not part of his daily routine, so he easily succumbed to the pressures from his soldiers and the prevailing circumstances that were upon him. If he had spent enough time with the LORD, he would have known His ways, and therefore, would have held His WORD in high esteem. If Saul had drawn nearer to the LORD, he would have been obedient to God, the Most High. Saul displayed weakness in time of adversity. This was the moment he was supposed to display able leadership and maturity, but failed miserably. "If you falter in times of trouble, how small is your strength!" (Proverbs 24:10). What a pity?

In the New Testament, Paul arrived in the city of Ephesus to the surprise of born-again believers. No one was expecting his arrival. Yet, he was overwhelmingly welcomed just like other preachers who passed through the city to proclaim the good news. With the burning desire to proclaim the WORD OF GOD, I believe, he might have immediately requested for the synagogue's location and its direction. His request was welcomed and was taken to the synagogue. At the synagogue, God performed marvelous miracles through him. It was beyond anyone's imagination. Even handkerchiefs that touched him were taken and placed on the sick, and they were instantly healed. This news conceivably spread throughout this bustling Ephesus city.

The seven sons of Sceva perhaps had seen or heard of these happenings. And they tried to replicate them but never knew the complexities involved in such ventures. One must be adequately prepared before stepping out to do the WORK OF GOD. There was no such preparation on their part before undertaking this daring exercise. So on that fateful day, they stepped out with the propensity to exorcise an evil spirit from a man possessed. The Bible says,

> Some Jews who went around driving out evil spirits tried to invoke the name of the Lord Jesus over those who were demon-possessed. They would say, "In the name of Jesus, whom Paul preaches, I command you to come out" (Acts 19:13).

But the evil spirit was bold enough to confront them.

> One day, the evil spirit answered them, 'Jesus I know, and I know about Paul, but who are you?' Then the man who had evil spirit jumped on them and overpowered them all. He gave them such a beating that they ran out the house naked and bleeding (Acts 19:15, 16).

## What is the Observation?

Here was a group of 'believers' driving out demons. Were they not doing the WORK OF GOD for which they must be rewarded? Yes, absolutely they were! Then why were they subdued and beaten by the evil spirit? Lack of the WORD OF GOD: pure and simple. They were not well equipped for this assignment. The devil is not scared of the WORK OF GOD. The WORK by itself cannot ward off evil spirits. Jesus is the embodiment of the WORD. Paul had spent so much time to study and know the WORD. That was why the spirit could testify about him and Jesus. This incident exposed their deficiency in the knowledge of the WORD OF GOD. How much time had they spent to study the WORD OF GOD? How often had they had communion with and in the presence of the Lord? The Founder of the Innerlife Chapel International church, once said, "Your depth in the WORD OF GOD determines your height in life" (Quist, 2014). This apathetic attitude of some pastors prompted Jesus to ask;

> Supposed one of you wants to build a tower. Will he not first sit down and estimate the cost to see if he has enough money to complete it? For if he lays the foundation and is not able to finish it, everyone who sees it will ridicule him, saying, 'This fellow began to build and was not able to finish.' Or suppose a king is about to go to war against another king. Will he not

first sit down and consider whether he is able with ten thousand men to oppose the one coming against him with twenty thousand? (Luke 14:28-31).

No! These individuals never conceived such an idea. As a result, I believe it never occurred to them to consider their spiritual standing before embarking on this assignment. These above mentioned mortal men were convinced their frequent and prompt presence in church services was enough for them to exorcise evil spirits. What a complete fallacy. Today, among members of our churches are those who nurture the same sentiments. They are not aware that

> ... our struggle is not against flesh and blood, but against the rulers, against the authorities, against the powers of this dark world and against the spiritual forces of evil in the heavenly realms (Ephesians 6:12).

The WORK OF GOD is not a business one should pay lip service to with hollow words and insincere respect or regard. It is the medium through which the WORD OF GOD reaches out to this ailing world. It is through the WORK OF GOD one's wealth of insight and enlightenment in the WORD OF GOD is exposed. The quality of the WORK OF GOD is influenced by the WORD OF GOD. For these facts, Satan (the devil) will do whatever he can to undermine its progress. But the WORD OF GOD and its design must grow, must spread and be protected. Therefore, it must be accorded the maximum attention it deserves. How can we achieve that feat? It is only by and through the WORD OF GOD, which is the Sword of the Spirit (Ephesians 6:17).

In His temptation in the wilderness, Jesus proved so well the difference and the relationship between the WORD and the WORK OF GOD. He, Himself being the WORD, knows how important the WORD is in our Christian journey. He was aware our spiritual war would be waged "against the rulers, against the authorities, against the powers of this dark world and against the spiritual forces of evil in the heavenly realms" (Ephesians 6:12). For these reasons, and others, He never hesitated to invoke it during the temptation by the tempter.

Jesus had been fasting for forty days and forty nights. Just like any human being, the Lord clothed Himself with human flesh and blood. He was therefore hungry after this spiritual exercise. The devil approached and tempted Jesus in His weakest moment. He took advantage of the opportunity to subject Him to his whims and caprices, yet Jesus prevailed. The trappings lacking in Jesus were the very ones Satan had tempted Him with. For three various times the tempter urged Him to do something against the WORD OF GOD.

In fact, Apostle Matthew recorded the thereby stating:

## The Word of God vs. the Work of God

If you are the Son of God,' he said, 'tell these stones to become bread'... 'If you are the Son Of God, he said, throw yourself down. For it is written: 'He will command his angels concerning you, and they will lift you up in their hands, so that you will not strike your foot against a stone" ... 'All this I will give you' he said, 'if you will bow down and worship me' (Matthew 4: 3, 6, 9).

Remember one thing here. Jesus Christ is the Son of God; the King of kings, the Lord of lords, the Alpha and Omega and the WORD incarnate, yet Satan had the guts to approach Him. Satan further gathered boldness enough to tempt Him. Will he not tempt you too? Do you think you are outside his scope of influence? Or, you are beyond the parameters of his wicked operations? No! Not in any way should you perceive such thoughts. Remember, Jesus warned His followers that "If they persecuted me, they will persecute you also" (John 15:20). In essence, if Satan was bold enough to tempt Jesus, he will not spare you from such machinations.

Jesus did not argue to prove His worth and status. He had all the necessary qualities to put them on display if He wanted too. Rather, He chose the most important weapon

What is the Observation?

we need to fight the devil and his cohorts: the WORD OF GOD.

He responded to his demands without any bit of flinch, as recorded in the gospel according to Saint Matthew, thus:

> It (the WORD OF GOD) is written: 'Man does not live on bread alone, but on every word that comes from the mouth of God'" ... 'It (WORD OF GOD) is also written: 'Do not put the Lord your God to test'... 'Away from me, Satan. For it (WORD OF GOD) is written: 'Worship the Lord your God, and serve him only' (Matthew 4:4, 7, 10).

Dear one, during their interaction, Jesus could have invoked His many titles: "...Wonderful Counselor, Mighty God, Everlasting Father, Prince of Peace" (Isaiah 9:6). He could also have insisted on: -

**His power**: "All authority in heaven and on earth has been given to me" (Matthew 28:18);

**His position**: He "...is at the right hand of God and is also interceding for us" (Romans 8:34);
**His possessions**: "Through him all things were made; without him nothing was made that has been made" (John 1:3) and

**His privilege**: "'Do not be afraid. I am the First and the Last'" (Revelations 1:17).
No! Jesus did neither of these. Instead, He used the WORD OF GOD as a weapon of defense to ward off Satan. He left this as an example for His followers.

Many 'mighty' men of God - and for that matter, women too - fell from grace to grass not because they had abandoned the LORD. No! They were still doing the WORK OF GOD. But the reason was that, they were so much immersed in the WORK OF GOD they drifted away from the WORD OF GOD to their own detriment. The WORD OF GOD is the foundation upon which the WORK OF GOD is built. It is the WORD OF GOD that solidly grounds the WORK OF GOD. The fact of the matter is the WORK OF GOD has its own plethora of problems. Yes, it does. Subsequently, it is the WORD OF GOD that would sustain the WORK OF GOD as it charts its way through its trying moments.

It is from the WORD that the worker draws encouragement, hope, confidence and faith to hold on till the WORK is ended. It is the WORD that shapes the attitude, behavior and character of the worker to make the WORK attractive and successful. It is still the WORD that causes one to be holy and righteous, dedicated and committed to the WORK. But with all these positive attributes, the WORD OF GOD hurts yet, at the same time, it heals the wounds it leaves along its path: both spiritual and emotional. However, no matter how, the WORD OF GOD must be held in high esteem.

# SIX

## What is the Response?

*"Do not let this <u>BOOK OF THE LAW</u> depart from your mouth, meditate on it day and night, so that you may be careful to do everything written it. Then you will be prosperous and successful"* (Joshua 1:8).

The charge to appoint God to write the kind of story we would want at the end of our individual lives rests on us. And the content of these stories would be determined by the priority we ascribe to either of these two delicate entities: the WORD OF GOD and the WORK OF GOD. One can choose to give the WORD precedence over the WORK OF GOD, or vice versa, at any given time. One can choose to align oneself to His WORD or reject its counsel. One can choose to be serious with the WORD or just pay lip service to its statutes and commandments. That game-changing decision depends on us. But there is a fundamental truth every Christian must be aware of; that in a particular day and time, His Son shall respond to a trumpet call just as God has said. This call shall wrap up events pertaining to our very existence on this earth. Apostle Paul related to this significant event with these words.

> For the Lord himself will come down from heaven, with a loud command, with the voice of an archangel and with a trumpet call of God, and the dead in Christ will rise first. After that, we who are still alive and are left will be caught up together with them in the clouds to meet the Lord in the air. And so we will be with the Lord forever (1 Thessalonians 4:16, 17).

This defining call and moment will bring time to a halt and God will give our lives His appraisal. It is therefore incumbent upon us to make the best out of this precious time we have been endowed with, by giving much attention to the WORD OF GOD. Jesus emphatically affirmed this certainty by saying; "Heaven and earth will pass away, but my WORDS (OF GOD) will never pass away" (Matthew 24:25). Yes, this declaration rings as true as the sun rising from the east and setting in the west.

## What is the response?

The WORD OF GOD and the WORK OF GOD cannot be isolated from each other at any given time. Where the WORD OF GOD is, the WORK OF GOD is also found. That is to say, the presence of the WORD OF GOD correspondingly creates a WORK OF GOD. That is why the WORK OF GOD's quality is measured, its parameter is determined and its definition is set by the WORD OF GOD. The basic truth undergirding this assessment is that, the WORK OF GOD is dependent upon the WORD OF GOD. This all-important truth is missing in the Christian community today. Painfully, some men and women of God have still not come to terms with this shortcoming. Instead, they stay far away from the WORD OF GOD without giving considerations to its residual effects. Some have become victims to these lapses at the end of the day, and paid for it dearly.

Pastor Jim Bakker is a living example of this experience. His infraction is a common phenomenon found among some men of God in our time. Their fame seems to have blurred the vision and the purpose for which they are called into the pastoral ministry.

Pastor Jim Bakker was a popular preacher, whose name was a household word in the world of televangelism. His innocent 'baby' face was a common feature on television in the 1980s through 1990s. His messages were a source of encouragement to the destitute, hope to the ostracized and uplifting for the down-trodden. His choice of words, and its attending eloquence, convincingly revealed his sincerity. The many followers, who glued their attention to their television sets so they could watch his program, were carried away by this rare gift he possessed. He took this advantage to promise his hearers massive returns on their 'spiritual investments' in his cause. His quest to leave a legacy worth talking about launched him into building what came to be known as 'PTL and Heritage USA' (PTL- Praise The Lord, a TV program and Heritage USA - a lodging for the contributors). In his own right, he was an icon in the Christian community in the United States, and further beyond its shores, until he had a sexual brush with a woman outside marriage. This twenty-minute escapade resulted in a revelation of a whole new dark world; a world that was at the blind side of his massive followers. The resulting outcome was devastating. It landed him in incarceration for approximately five years. This was the price Pastor Jim Bakker dearly paid for drifting away from the WORD OF GOD when he concentrated heavily, extensively and exclusively on the WORK OF GOD. Jim expressed his mistakes and regrets in these words:-

## What is the response?

God put me in prison so I could study His Word, get to know Him, and learn the meaning of forgiveness. Had I been seeking God daily, studying the Bible, and living by its principles all along as we built PTL and Heritage USA, I have no doubt that I would never have gone to prison. I would have seen the error of my ways reflected in God's Word, and I would have taken the appropriate corrective measures. But because I had allowed my relationship with God to grow cold and had ignored His Word, God put me in a position in which I had only two choices – either get it right with God, or die (Bakker, 1996).

I doff my hat for Pastor Jim Bakker for coming to terms with himself, and the knowledge he gained while he was behind bars. He never blamed nor accused anyone for his predicament. He accepted full responsibility for his wrongful decisions. He learned a simple lesson the hard way. So from this teachable, but unbearable scandal, he made this observation:-

The most important change I would make is this: I would not emphasize the physical structure, but I would encourage people to fall in love with Jesus. I always felt that Heritage USA was merely the box in which we packaged the gospel, a big box, a beautiful box, but just a box, nonetheless. Unfortunately, the box began to get more attention than the gift inside. Eventually, we spent so much time, energy, and money trying to build a bigger, better box we neglected the priceless gift of Jesus Christ. If I could somehow be transported back in time to PTL in the 1980s, I would keep my attention off the physical, material plant, the place known as Heritage USA, and keep my eyes on Jesus (Bakker, 1996).

This unfortunate incident caused so much uproar in the Christian community. It shook its very foundation to the core. It was an incident that its rippling effect reached farther than deemed possible. But, even after this much-publicized news, some men of God had not heeded to the warnings so they could refrain from the dangers involved. Instead of pursuing the Blesser, who would sustain us during our turbulent times, we are pursuing the blessings at the expense of our spiritual growth and its obligations.

There is no proper mechanism in place to measure the minister's pursuit of God through His WORD. And the man of God has no one to set parameters within which to function. For that matter, complacency is easily entrenched. The man of God sets his own time and space to operate. He is his own boss and therefore, there is no one in particular

## What is the response?

to responsibly hold him accountable. This attitude then paves way for the man of God to pour much energy and time into his own written agenda. The most important priority - the pursuit of God through His WORD and prayer - is left to the backburner. When the day is over, this minister would pause to evaluate his own work. He would definitely congratulate himself for the day's work well done. There is no one to evaluate his performance and check his spiritual growth in order that any shortcoming could be pointed out.

These infractions usually perch at the blind side of the congregation's eye. Some members also, not aware of the man of God's attitude, would use physical things: gigantic church building, size of the congregation, many departments and committees, popularity and others as the scale to weigh his progress. Therefore, when the man of God is drifting away from the WORD OF GOD, it is difficult for him, and even those around him, to realize. Some have surrounded themselves with individuals who would only highlight their physical achievements and sing their praises. It is equally hard for those outside this 'exclusive club' who would realize these shortcomings to caution when aware of. This behavior creates a recipe for disaster as time goes by.

The WORD OF GOD cannot and must not be compromised. Neither the man of God for a moment should marginalize or ostracize the WORD OF GOD. Should such a scenario occur, questions should be asked, "are the damages not going to be so devastating that they could not be easily controlled?" The man of God is required to spend more time with the WORD and in prayer than any other demand on his agenda. This endeavor must be coupled with fasting and meditation. The WORK OF GOD can be delegated to someone else. With proper orientation, explanation and direction, the WORK OF GOD could and would be performed perfectly to its specific requirements by this person. It is not so with the study of the WORD OF GOD and with prayers. If we do not take time to study and pray, we will not know the will of God. In fact, every minister must make diligent efforts to study and pray so he could be approved as one who "correctly handles the WORD of truth" (2Timothy 2:15).

Peter confirmed this truth, saying; "We will turn this responsibility (WORK OF GOD) over to them and will give attention to prayer and the ministry of the WORD" (Acts 6:3, 4). For effective ministry Jesus advised that before the believer steps out, he must prepare adequately behind closed doors. One must immerse himself deeply in the WORD OF GOD.

## What is the response?

In his work in *They Spoke from God*, the writer notes as the following,

> The true God speaks and reveals himself to people; he wants to have a relationship with all who are willing. The Bible is his WORD given to people *through* people, so he can be known and his love experienced (Cotton, 2003).

God wants us to know Him, and know Him beyond the realms of our needs and wants. Armed with this knowledge, the believer can cope in any trying moment. No matter what, these trying moments will come as we perform His good work. The WORD OF GOD is the only source of solace for the worker. The WORD should be the believer's road map. It must be consulted frequently. There should be no room given to creating a distance between it and the believer in any moment. In bad and good times, the WORD OF GOD should be as close to the believer as possible.

# Epilogue

*"I have hidden your <u>WORD</u> in my heart that I might not sin against you"* (Psalm 119:11).

The question of the difference and the relationship between the WORD OF GOD and the WORK OF GOD had hooked me on for a long time. A kind of 'spiritual addiction' you would want to call it. This kept my whole life on edge as I wondered why the WORD OF GOD is not treasured. But this intense urging began to subside when I made the initial effort to research the difference and the relationship between the WORD OF GOD and the WORK OF GOD and write the result in this book for all.

It all began after observing the attitude some believers fondly display toward the WORD OF GOD. These folks fail to value its benefits in their lives as Christians. It then started to take a toll on me. I could not fathom anyone paying lip service to the WORD OF GOD. I concluded after this critical observation that, the majority of the Christian community are more interested in doing the WORK OF GOD - which is more visible and therefore would attract frequent praises - than listening to the WORD OF GOD should they run upon each other. It has been an issue that had disconcerted me for days and nights without number. After wrestling with it, I felt the urge to find the answer from the Bible. I believe with every fiber of my being that the Bible has an answer - directly or indirectly - to every question we might encounter in life. For the power of the WORD OF GOD and the power of God Himself have transcended age and time and this power has transformed so many lives which I have come to know over the years.

I am not, in any way, attempting to play down the importance of the WORK OF GOD, and so elevate the WORD OF GOD above it in this book. It will do a great disservice to the Christian community should I make such an attempt. In fact, through the WORK OF GOD many Christians have come to see the ministration and manifestation of the power of the WORD OF GOD. The WORK OF GOD done within the parameters of the church, just like the non-religious ones we do outside the

## Epilogue

church, has its fair share of problems. These problems - lack of respect from church members, lateness, being irresponsible - will confront the believer. However difficult or not these problems might be, the WORK OF GOD must move on and be sustained. That strength and tenacity to sustain it will be drawn only from the WORD OF GOD. But should they converge at a place and time, what should the believer do? This is where the WORD OF GOD takes precedence over the WORK OF GOD.

Here is a story where the WORK OF GOD was the medium through which the WORD OF GOD was channeled. It occurred in a place no one ever suspected it would. But it did and brought glory and honor to God.

Sami is stout and bulgy. Compared to others, his shoulders looked a bit square. When exchanging greetings with a fellow Christian, his smile is flavored with love and joy. He flashes this infectious smile across his face with ease. His intention for the WORK OF GOD is flawless. He loves the Lord so much that, he does not care about his life. Where others are scared to venture, there he is to volunteer and work for the Lord. It was evident when fellow Christians visited from the United States. His ministry spanned the days of the Lebanese war. Yet under these critical circumstances, Sami availed himself for the Lord. His friend, Brother Franklin Graham described their experience thus:

> For the next several days, I accompanied Sami around Beirut. The whole city was in chaos. Sami's immediate concern was the families of his church. Time and time again, he risked his life - and mine too - as we delivered food to their homes under a rain of bullets (Graham, 1995).

Sami Dagher epitomizes Jesus' exhortation to the disciples that were following Him one afternoon.

> If anyone comes to me and does not hate his father and mother, his wife and children, his brothers and sisters - yes even his own life - he cannot be my disciple. Anyone who does not carry his cross and follow me cannot be my disciple (Luke 14:26, 27).

Sami is a Lebanese Christian whose story was told to an audience by Dr. Ravi Zacharias. Sami's wife accompanied him on a risky adventure and was full of praise for him from what she experienced. In fact, she was shocked when Sami defied the odds to do what was beyond human comprehension. He wanted to obey the Lord and his kind gesture paid off tremendously at long last. Through this act

# Epilogue

of kindness, he caused a rich Lebanese business family to make bold decision for the Lord.

This man was a businessman, who lost a briefcase full of money along a Lebanese highway. Sami and his wife, Joy traveled the same route. They happened to be the ones who came across the lost briefcase. Under the prevailing violent circumstances ravaging this once peaceful nation Sami should not have considered stopping. Joy pestered her loving husband to refrain from his intentions, yet he failed to accept her piece of advice. Without any resignation, he stopped and picked the briefcase to satisfy his soul.

After they got home, Sami ravaged through the briefcase with quiet intention. He found a complimentary card in there. He put in a call to the number on the card. The response was from a man who confirmed his ownership. Sami then quickly assured him of the safety of the briefcase and its contents. They arranged to meet so this rightful owner could collect his prized possession.

When they had met, according to Ravi, Sami gave the man his missing possession. With shaking hands, this owner opened his briefcase and checked the content to make sure everything was intact. When he had satisfied himself, he dipped his hand into it and gathered as much money as his both hands could contain. Then he gave everything to Sami, but Sami refused. Sami said he doesn't take offering except on Sunday. Sami invited this man to church. And to their utmost surprise, the businessman came the ensuing Sunday with all his family members. Sami took the opportunity after their fruitful interaction to lead this beautiful family to the Lord (Zacharias, 2014).

Of course, there may be some exceptions where the believer might be under intense urging of the Holy Spirit to go and do the WORK OF GOD. However, I believe these situations are rare. From my personal experience as a minister of the gospel, I learned to devote much time to the WORD OF GOD. I am doing the WORK OF GOD as a teacher too. At no time did I ever compromise the study of the WORD OF GOD. It had helped me to build good relationships with the Holy Spirit and those around.

Beloved, would you pause and ponder over the journey you took with me through this book? Ponder over the difference and the relationship between the WORD OF GOD and the WORK OF GOD. I urge you to ponder over my observations, over my response and draw your own personal conclusions. However, I will suggest never ever to be more strongly drawn to the WORK OF GOD than it should be with the WORD OF GOD. But do not marginalize the WORK OF GOD either. It is as important as the WORD

## Epilogue

OF GOD. The fact is the two cannot be done at the same time. One must precede the other: the WORD OF GOD must surely do the WORK OF GOD. With this mindset, let us also take advantage of the prevailing abundance of biblical information to assist us in the study the WORD OF GOD. If we fail to avail ourselves to these intense studies, time would conspire against us and the purpose for which we have been called could falter.

Thank you for buying this book and the precious time you spent reading this material. I truly appreciate the effort you have made. Upon this note, I will urge you to make reading the WORD OF GOD your daily priority. For "There is a way that seems right to a man, but in the end it leads to death" (Proverbs 14:12). The WORD OD GOD will take you away from this kind of way if you would commit yourself to spending more time with it. God richly bless you.

## Impressions about the Bible (Word Of God) by some Prominent Persons:

"It is impossible to rightly govern a nation without God and the Bible (WORD OF GOD)."

**George Washington**

..................................

"A thorough knowledge of the Bible (WORD OF GOD) is worth more than a college education."

**Theodore Roosevelt**

..................................

"All the miseries and evils which men suffer from vice, crime, ambition, injustice, oppression, slavery and war, proceed from their despising or neglecting the precepts contained in the Bible (WORD OF GOD)."

**Noah Webster**

..................................

"Hold fast to the Bible (WORD OF GOD). To the influence of this Book we are indebted for all the progress made in true civilization and to this we must look as our guide in the future."

**Ulysses Grant**

..................................

"Put your nose into the Bible (WORD OF GOD) every day. It is your spiritual food. And then share it. Make a vow not to be a lukewarm Christian."

**Kirk Cameron**

..................................

"The Bible (WORD OF GOD) is one of the greatest blessings bestowed by God on the children of men. It has God for its author; salvation for its end, and truth without any mixture for its matter. It is all pure."

**John Locke**

..................................

"The Bible (WORD OF GOD) is proved to be a revelation from God, by the reasonableness and holiness of its precepts; all its commands, exhortations, and promises having the most direct tendency to make men wise, holy, and happy in themselves, and useful to one another."

**Adam Clarke**

..................................

"The Bible (WORD OF GOD) is the rock on which this Republic rests."

**Andrew Jackson**

..................................

Impressions about the Bible (Word Of God) by some Prominent Persons

"The Christian's Bible (WORD OF GOD) is a drug store. Its contents remain the same, but the medical practice changes."

**Mark Twain**

..........................................

"The book to read is not the one which thinks for you, but the one which makes you think. No book in the world equals the Bible (WORD OF GOD) for that."

**Harper Lee**

........................................

"The rivers of America will run with blood filled to their banks before we will submit to them taking the Bible (WORD OF GOD) out of our schools."

**Billy Sunday**

*** (Brainy Media, 2012)

# References

Bakker, J. (1996), *I WAS WRONG*, Nashville, TN: Thomas Nelson, Inc., p. 350, p. 470.

Brainy Media, (2012), *Various famous persons*. Retrieved April 28, 2012 from http://www.brainyquote.com/quotes/authors.html

Cotton, R. (2003). God Reveals Himself to His People. In William C. Williams (Vol. Ed.), *They Spoke from God*, Springfield, MO: Gospel Publishing House, p 266.

Graham, F. (1995). *REBEL WITH A CAUSE*, Nashville, TN: Thomas Nelson, p. 195.

Quist, J. A. (Preacher). (2014). *Make full proof of your ministry*. Bronx, NY: Innerlife Chapel International.

Tenney, M.C. & Douglas, J. D. (Eds.) (1963). Word. In M.C. Tenney & J. D. Douglas, *New international Bible dictionary* (2nd ed., p. 1068). Grand Rapids, MI: Zondervan.

Williams, J. R. (1996). *Renewal Theology*, Grand Rapids, MI: Zondervan, p. 30.

Zacharias, R. (Speaker). (2014) *A robust Christianity amidst today's challenges*. Retrieved December 24, 2014 from http://www.youtube.com

# The Word of God vs. the Work of God

www.ingramcontent.com/pod-product-compliance
Lightning Source LLC
Chambersburg PA
CBHW070915160426
43193CB00011B/1474